# BORDERLINE CASE

## International Tax Policy, Corporate Research and Development, and Investment

~~Withdrawn~~

*Edited by*

JAMES M. POTERBA

Board on Science, Technology, and Economic Policy

National Research Council

NATIONAL ACADEMY PRESS
Washington, D.C. 1997

**NATIONAL ACADEMY PRESS • 2101 Constitution Ave., N.W. • Washington, D.C. 20418**

NOTICE: The conference from which the papers in this publication were drawn was approved by the Governing Board of the National Research Council, whose members come from the councils of the National Academy of Sciences, the National Academy of Engineering, and the Institute of Medicine. The members of the board responsible for the project were chosen for their special competences and with regard for appropriate balance.

This publication was supported by the National Aeronautics and Space Administration and the National Science Foundation. Program support for the Board on Science, Technology, and Economic Policy is provided by a grant from the Alfred P. Sloan Foundation

**Library of Congress Cataloging-in-Publication Data**

Borderline case : international tax policy, corporate research and
    development, and investment / Board on Science, Technology, and
    Economic Policy, National Research Council ; James M. Poterba,
    Editor.
        p.   cm.
    Papers presented at a conference held at the National Academy of
Sciences in Washington, D.C., on February 14, 1997.
    Includes bibliographical references and index.
    ISBN 0-309-06368-X
    1. International business enterprises—Taxation—United States—
Congresses.  2. Research, Industrial—Taxation—United States—
Congresses.  3. Research and development tax credit—United States—
Congresses.  4. Capital investments—United States—Congresses.
I. Poterba, James M.  II. National Research Council (U.S.).  Board
on Science, Technology, and Economic Policy.  III. Series.
HD2753.U6B64    1998
336.24'3'0973—dc21                                      97-45343
                                                           CIP

*Cover:* The emblem appearing on the cover of this publication is an illustration of the bronze medallion in the floor of the Great Hall in the National Academy of Sciences building in Washington, D.C. The medallion is the wellhead placed in the floor when the spectroscopic case over which the Foucault pendulum swings is lowered below the floor level. The design is based on a map of the solar system published in 1661 by Andreas Cellarius Palatinus. The array of planets is the Copernican system as know to Galileo.

Copyright 1997 by the National Academy of Sciences. All rights reserved.

Printed in the United States of America

# NATIONAL RESEARCH COUNCIL

## BOARD ON SCIENCE, TECHNOLOGY, AND ECONOMIC POLICY

A. MICHAEL SPENCE, *Chairman*
Dean, Graduate School of Business
Stanford University

RUBEN METTLER, *Vice Chairman*
Chairman and CEO (retired)
TRW, Inc.

M. KATHY BEHRENS
Managing Partner
Robertson, Stephens & Company

WILLIAM J. SPENCER
Chairman
SEMATECH

JAMES F. GIBBONS
Professor of Electrical Engineering
Stanford University

JOSEPH E. STIGLITZ
Senior Vice President and Chief
    Economist
The World Bank

GEORGE N. HATSOPOULOS
President and CEO
Thermo Electron Corporation

ALAN WM. WOLFF
Managing Partner
Dewey Ballantine

DALE JORGENSON
Frederic Eaton Abbe Professor
    of Economics
Harvard University

*Ex-Officio Members*

BRUCE M. ALBERTS
President
National Academy of Sciences

RALPH LANDAU
Consulting Professor Economics
Stanford University

JAMES T. LYNN
Advisor
Lazard Freres

WILLIAM A. WULF
President
National Academy of Engineering

KENNETH I. SHINE
President
Institute of Medicine

BURTON J. McMURTRY
General Partner
Technology Venture Investors

MARK B. MYERS
Senior Vice President
Xerox Corporation

*Staff*

STEPHEN A. MERRILL
Executive Director

JAMES M. POTERBA
Professor of Economics
Massachusetts Institute of
    Technology

CHARLES W. WESSNER
Program Director

PAUL ROMER
Professor of Economics
Graduate School of Business
Stanford University

LENA J. LAWRENCE
Administrative Assistant

# STEERING COMMITTEE ON TAXATION OF U.S. ENTERPRISES

JAMES M. POTERBA, *Chair*
Professor of Economics
Massachusetts Institute of
  Technology

JAMES R. HINES, JR.
Professor of Business Economics
  and Public Policy
University of Michigan

R. GLENN HUBBARD
Russell L. Carson Professor of
  Economics and Finance
Graduate School of Business
Columbia University

DALE JORGENSON
Frederic Eaton Abbe Professor of
  Economics
Harvard University

RUBEN METTLER
Chairman and CEO (retired)
TRW, Inc.

PETER E. NUGENT
Vice President, Controller
Merck & Company

RAYMOND J. WIACEK
Partner
Jones, Day, Reavis and Pogue


STEPHEN A. MERRILL
Project Director

# Contents

# Preface

In 1991 the National Academies of Sciences and Engineering established the Board on Science, Technology, and Economic Policy as a forum in which economists, technologists, scientists, financial and management experts, and policymakers could broaden and deepen understanding of the relationships between science and technology and economic performance. In its first three years, the Board's activities focused on the adequacy and efficiency of public and private domestic investment in physical and human capital. The Board's first report, *Investing for Productivity and Prosperity,* underscored the need for higher rates of national saving and investment. Its principal recommendation was to shift the base for taxation from income to consumption.

In the past two years, the Board has turned its attention to more microeconomic concerns—technology policies broadly defined and their relationship to international trade relations, determinants of competitive performance in a wide range of manufacturing and service industries, and changes in patterns of R&D and innovation investments. A series of conferences, workshops, and reports, of which this volume is the second, comprises the latter body of STEP work entitled *U.S. Industry: Restructuring and Renewal* because it represents a broad assessment of U.S. industrial performance in an international context at a time of domestic economic confidence and optimism but uncertainty about the consequences of fundamental changes in the composition of the economy and processes of innovation. Other publications under this title will include reports of workshops on measurement of industrial research and innovation, commissioned papers on a dozen industries, a review of trends in financing new technology-based enterprises, and the conclusions and recommendations of the Board. This series of projects would not have been possible without the financial support of the

National Aeronautics and Space Administration and National Science Foundation and the personal encouragement of Daniel Goldin, NASA Administrator.

With the exception of the Introduction, the papers in this volume were presented at a conference, "International Tax Policy, Corporate Research and Development, and Investment," held at the National Academy of Sciences in Washington, D.C., on February 14, 1997. The conference was organized by a committee chaired by James Poterba, STEP member and professor of economics at M.I.T., and included James Hines of the University of Michigan (at the time of the conference, Harvard University Kennedy School of Government), Glenn Hubbard of Columbia University, Peter Nugent of Merck and Company, and Raymond Wiacek of Jones, Day, Reavis and Pogue, in addition to STEP members Dale Jorgenson and Ruben Mettler.

The papers prepared for and the commentaries presented at the conference persuasively make the point that U.S. international tax rules and tax treatment of corporate research and development have important economic consequences through their influence on the investment decisions of multinational companies that account for most of the R&D performed in and most of the goods and services exported from the United States. Yet these policies have not been consistent but subject to the vagaries of federal budget and partisan politics. They deserve more thoughtful attention from policymakers, both in the context of incremental changes in the income tax system and in the consideration of fundamental tax reform.

We are grateful to the organizers of the conference, the contributors to and reviewers of this volume, and other participants in the meeting. We wish to acknowledge a special debt to Ray Wiacek and his colleagues at Jones, Day for technical assistance in preparing the manuscript and glossary, which we hope will assist readers in understanding a complex subject.

A. MICHAEL SPENCE
*Chairman*

STEPHEN A. MERRILL
*Executive Director*

The **National Academy of Sciences** is a private, nonprofit, self-perpetuating society of distinguished scholars engaged in scientific and engineering research, dedicated to the furtherance of science and technology and to their use for the general welfare. On the authority of the charter granted to it by Congress in 1863, the Academy has a working mandate that requires it to advise the federal government on scientific and technical matters. Dr. Bruce M. Alberts is president of the National Academy of Sciences.

The **National Academy of Engineering** was established in 1964, under the charter of the National Academy of Sciences, as a parallel organization of outstanding engineers. It is autonomous in its administration and in the selection of members, sharing with the National Academy of Sciences the responsibility for advising the federal government. The National Academy of Engineering also sponsors engineering programs aimed at meeting national needs, encourages education and research, and recognizes the superior achievements of engineers. Dr. William A. Wulf is president of the National Academy of Engineering.

The **Institute of Medicine** was established in 1970 by the National Academy of Sciences to secure the services of eminent members of appropriate professions in the examination of policy matters pertaining to the health of the public. The institute acts under the responsibility given to the National Academy of Sciences by its congressional charter to be an adviser to the federal government and, upon its own initiative, to identify issues of medical care, research, and education. Dr. Kenneth I. Shine is the president of the Institute of Medicine.

The **National Research Council** was organized by the National Academy of Sciences in 1916 to associate the broad community of science and technology with the Academy's purposes of furthering knowledge and advising the federal government. Functioning in accordance with general policies determined by the Academy, the council has become the principal operating agency of both the National Academy of Sciences and the National Academy of Engineering in providing services to the government, the public, and the scientific and engineering communities. The council is administered jointly by both academies and the Institute of Medicine. Dr. Bruce M. Alberts and Dr. William A. Wulf are chairman and vice chairman, respectively, of the National Research Council.

# Introduction

JAMES POTERBA
*Massachusetts Institute of Technology*

The global business environment is changing. Even as recently as 10 years ago, international joint ventures were relatively uncommon, and large U.S.-based multinational corporations could be considered "American firms." Yet the growing integration of world markets for capital and many products, coupled with the rise of electronic communication media such as e-mail and video teleconferencing, has made it more difficult to assign corporations to particular countries. The emergence of "virtual corporations," which raise capital in one country, carry out research in another, manufacture in a third, and finally sell their products in a fourth country, is an important reality of the 1990s. Large U.S.-based "virtual firms" in many industries now compete with similar virtual firms based in other nations. The identification of firms as "American," "Dutch," or "Japanese" may now reflect little more than an accident of birth. Current indications suggest that the trend toward global firms will continue and, if anything, accelerate in the future.

One of the few features of the business environment that *does* depend on where a firm is nominally headquartered is its tax treatment. The U.S. corporation income tax is a "residence-based" tax, which means that U.S. firms are taxed on their worldwide income. Since U.S.-based firms often pay taxes to foreign governments on profits earned abroad, the U.S. tax code includes a foreign tax credit provision that allows U.S.-based firms to reduce their U.S. tax liability by the amount of foreign tax payments, subject to a variety of limitations. Firms that are constrained by these limits and pay more foreign taxes than they can credit against U.S. tax liability become excess foreign tax credit firms, a condition that can affect their incentives for domestic as well as foreign investment and R&D expenditure. A further complication arises because U.S.-based firms are taxed on the earnings of their foreign subsidiaries only when these earnings are repatriated to the U.S. parent firm. U.S. taxes can therefore be deferred when profits are earned in a low-tax foreign country, retained within the subsidiary, and rein-vested.

The core of the tax code as it relates to international operations of U.S.-based firms is a set of provisions that defines taxable income and the tax burdens on domestic and foreign business. Two principal sets of rules concern the deferral of tax on income earned abroad and the allocation of joint costs, such as headquarters staff or R&D expenses, across operations in different countries. The first set of provisions, known as "anti-deferral rules," arises because the U.S. tax system does not generally tax multinational firms on their income from foreign operations until the earnings from these operations are repatriated to the United States. By retaining earnings in a foreign subsidiary, a U.S.-based firm can therefore defer U.S. tax on these earnings. A variety of tax rules, many of which have been enacted in the last decade, limit the extent of income tax deferral on foreign earnings. These rules require U.S.-based firms to include part of their foreign profits in their current taxable income and consequently can raise the effective tax buô en on foreign operations. These rules can, in some cases, also raise the effective tax burdens on the domestic source income of foreign members of U.S.-based multinationals. The anti-deferral rules in the United States stand in marked contrast to the tax rules in many other developed nations, a number of which do not tax the foreign-source earnings of their domestic multinationals at all.

The second set of core international tax provisions, known as "allocation rules," governs the extent to which U.S. group expenses are allocated to and deducted against reported foreign-source taxable earnings. These rules are particularly important with respect to R&D outlays and other spending on intangible assets, because they reduce the foreign tax credits that may be claimed as an offset against the U.S. taxes imposed on reported taxable income of U.S.-based multinationals. The R&D allocation rules generally increase the after-tax cost of carrying out research and development in the United States, and they can place U.S.-based firms at a disadvantage relative to firms based in other nations. Anti-deferral rules and allocation provisions substantially complicate administration of the U.S. corporate income tax and can also affect the incentives for plant, equipment, and R&D investment by U.S.-based multinational firms.

The complexity of various international tax rules and the relatively small number of firms affected by them have limited the attention that they have received in discussions of national policy toward science, technology, and capital formation. To remedy this situation, the National Research Council's Board on Science, Technology, and Economic Policy (STEP) organized a conference to consider the impact of these provisions. The meeting, held at the National Academy of Sciences in Washington on February 14, 1997, brought together industry experts from large multinational firms, academic researchers who have explored the quantitative impact of tax provisions on corporate R&D spending, and tax policy experts able to place the international tax rules in a broader context of options for tax reform. This volume, containing the papers and prepared comments presented at the conference, provides background material on the structure of international tax rules and the provisions of the tax code affecting corporate R&D performed in the United States, as well as downstream investment in plant and equipment.

My attempt in this introduction to summarize the papers and discussion does not purport to represent the views of the STEP Board or the consensus conclusions and recommendations of the National Research Council. Rather, this material will be one of several elements to be considered by the STEP Board early next year in its formal report of a study of the changes in industrial R&D and innovation and their bearing on industries' performance. That study and these conference proceedings have been supported by the National Aeronautics and Space Administration and the National Science Foundation.

Taken together, the presentations to the conference suggest that these tax rules significantly affect the business environment for R&D spending and investment in physical capital, and they raise a number of issues that warrant further attention from tax policymakers. International tax rules primarily affect firms that carry out business in several nations. Although such firms represent a minority of corporations, they account for more than *three-quarters* of corporate R&D spending in the United States. Changes in these tax provisions therefore have the potential to exert first-order influence on the level, location, and composition of research and development spending.

Industry experts from large, R&D-intensive, multinational firms argued that international tax rules can and do affect the effective tax burden on research and innovation expenditure and on the follow-on physical investment that embodies the outcomes of this R&D. They affect the incentives for firms to carry out research and to invest in physical capital in other nations, because foreign operations can have immediate consequences for the firm's corporation tax liability in the United States. International tax rules can also affect the tax burdens that multinational firms face on purely domestic projects. For some firms, these rules raise the cost of carrying out research and development projects *in the United States*. The effects of international tax rules on aggregate R&D spending in the United States are difficult to quantify. Industry experts acknowledge that the location of many corporate R&D facilities is driven by the availability of skilled researchers rather than tax policy considerations. They also indicate, however, that when other factors are equal, tax disparities can affect the size and location of R&D facilities.

In analyzing tax incentives for plant and equipment investment or R&D outlays, it is important to consider the tax burdens on U.S.-based firms relative to those of their competitors. Where multinational firms based in other nations face lower tax burdens on operations in the United States or elsewhere, U.S.-based firms may choose not to invest in projects that other multinationals find attractive to undertake. In some cases this occurs because the international tax provisions of the U.S. tax code raise the effective tax rates on U.S.-based firms.

The precise effect of international tax rules on the incentives facing a firm depends on the nature of the corporation's multinational operations, the particular countries in which the firm has operations, and a range of other firm-specific characteristics. Several conference participants observed that it is essential to recognize firm heterogeneity with respect to these rules. Changes in the tax rules that reduce the cost of R&D projects for some firms may increase the cost of similar projects for others.

The discussion of how international tax rules affect individual firm decision making provides an important warrant for studying these public policy questions, but it does not lead naturally to quantitative evidence on how these tax rules and other tax incentives affect total private R&D outlays and private investment spending. To address these issues, the STEP Board commissioned summary papers from several leading academic researchers who have studied the influence of taxation on corporate R&D and plant and equipment investment. Although international tax rules were largely ignored in academic discussions of tax policy until the early 1980s, in the last decade and a half there has been a substantial volume of research on these issues, and this work provides further evidence of the importance of these rules in affecting firm behavior.

The existing scholarly literature makes two important observations about the impact of international tax provisions. First, because the location of some R&D facilities and some types of manufacturing facilities may be largely independent of other business considerations, such decisions can be very sensitive to tax rate differences or other factors that create cost differentials between different locations. An example of such facilities might be late-stage pharmaceutical manufacturing plants, which do not depend on access to a highly skilled work force. Firms considering the construction of such facilities are likely to be very attuned to the impact of taxation on the net cost of operations. For footloose facilities, one would expect a priori to find a high "supply elasticity" with respect to tax incentives, and there is a presumption that tax differentials either between firms or across countries would have notable consequences for the location of such activities.

Second, the empirical literature on international tax rules and the level and location of business activity yields substantial evidence that tax rules have important effects. Expenditures on R&D by multinational firms respond to tax rate differentials, with many estimates suggesting that a 1 percentage point increase in the cost of an R&D project reduces expenditures on that type of project by more than 1 percent. The question of whether private R&D spending is highly sensitive to its after-tax cost is an important consideration with regard to the desirability of special tax subsidies. If the percentage increase in R&D spending exceeds the percentage reduction in the cost per unit of R&D, then a tax credit that costs $100 million will increase private R&D spending by more than this amount. Empirical evidence on tax incentives and R&D suggests that the variation in the cost of R&D induced by international tax rules could have important effects on the aggregate volume of R&D spending. This evidence also suggests that well-designed R&D tax incentives, which reduce the effective cost of carrying out corporate R&D, have substantial power to increase private R&D outlays.

Evidence on whether and how international tax rules affect the pattern of foreign direct investment (FDI) and the location of manufacturing facilities is less robust than is the evidence with regard to R&D. This may reflect the fact that much FDI is motivated by strategic business considerations that override tax-related international differences in R&D costs. One striking piece of evidence on how taxation affects business location comes from the location decisions of in-bound FDI, that is, investment in U.S. facilities by foreign multinationals. The pattern of state-level corporate income taxes in the United States appears to affect the location patterns of such inbound FDI. Given the small differentials among these tax rates, it seems likely that the larger cross-national variations in corporate income tax also affect investment location decisions. Another important finding that confirms the impact of international tax rules on firm behavior concerns interest allocation rules. Firms that face higher after-tax costs of borrowing in the United States borrow less and are more likely to configure their financial structure in alternative ways that preserve interest-tax deductions

An important open issue with respect to tax rates, R&D outlays, and physical investment concerns the degree to which changes in the location of R&D facilities affect the location of follow-on manufacturing facilities. There appears to be substantial variation across industries, and even across manufacturing processes, in the links among basic research, development, and subsequent manufacturing operations. Although one industry expert cited an example of a pharmaceutical firm whose manufacturing plant location was determined largely by the previous location of R&D facilities, other types of manufacturing processes appear to be more easily separated from earlier development facilities.

It is difficult to discuss detailed tax provisions, such as those in the international tax arena without discussing potential tax reform. Tax reform raises two distinct issues. The first concerns the impact of fundamental tax reform—for example replacing U.S. corporate and personal income taxes with a value-added tax on the incentives for R&D and plant and equipment investment by U.S.-based multinational firms. The second concerns potential changes in the current income tax code, short of replacing the corporate income tax, that might stimulate R&D spending and capital formation generally.

Fundamental tax reform would have many different effects on the tax treatment of physical and technological investment by U.S.-based firms. Such reform would remove some tax provisions that currently favor R&D spending relative to other types of investment, notably the immediate expensing of R&D and the incremental research and experimentation tax credit. Fundamental tax reform would also affect the tax treatment of royalty income received by U.S. multinationals that license technology abroad and would eliminate the R&D expense allocation rules that are necessitated by the current income tax. The net effect of these multiple reforms is highly dependent on firm circumstances. At least for some firms that are currently able to take full advantage of tax incentives for R&D activity, fundamental tax reform could reduce the attractiveness of R&D spending. Effects on physical investment incentives are also complicated, but because most plant and equipment investment is not eligible for expensing at the present time, moving toward a consumption tax would be more likely to increase investment incentives.

The chances of fundamental tax reform are always quite low, and most discussions of tax reform therefore focus on incremental changes that might be made in the federal corporation income tax. Several reform proposals were outlined and evaluated at the meeting. Industry participants emphasized the need for more stability in the tax code. A very common complaint about the latest incremental research and experimentation credit, which expired on May 31, 1997, but has been extended retroactively, is that its short-term character reduces its impact on R&D spending. R&D programs, particularly those that focus on basic research, inherently represent long-term commitments of corporate resources. Executives considering such expenditure programs are understandably reluctant to increase R&D budgets in response to a credit that has a legislated life far shorter than their R&D program and could fail to be extended. Stable, long-term rules for the tax treatment of R&D expenditures thus command widespread support in the business community as a policy reform that would encourage corporate spending on research and development.

A second incremental tax reform proposal concerns the statutory corporation tax rate in the United States. A number of tax practitioners at the conference suggested that the current statutory rate of 35 percent is high relative to rates in other major industrial countries and that this tax rate places U.S.-based firms at a competitive disadvantage relative to other global firms. Recent history may be helpful in evaluating this claim. When the Tax Reform Act of 1986 was adopted, the federal statutory corporate income tax rate fell from 46 to 34 percent. This reduction transformed the United States into a relatively "low-tax" developed country and made it attractive for many firms to report earned income in the United States rather than other, higher-taxed jurisdictions. In the decade since the watershed tax reform of 1986, however, other developed nations have modified their tax codes, and as a result, U.S.-based firms no longer enjoy a statutory tax rate well below that of other countries. The statutory tax rate in the United States also depends on the combined federal and state income tax rates. Firms based in most other nations face only a single, national level of taxation.

One of the crucial lessons from the economic theory of investment behavior is that the statutory corporate tax rate is not a sufficient measure of the tax burden facing corporate outlays on plant, equipment, or R&D. Rather, the effective tax burden depends on the statutory tax rate as well as the provisions for depreciating physical capital goods, the tax treatment of interest and dividend payments, and a host of more specialized provisions such as the corporate alternative minimum tax and the treatment of foreign-source income. Although comparisons of statutory corporate tax rates in different nations are simple, they provide an imperfect measure of the tax burdens on both tangible and intangible investments across countries. Nevertheless, the shifting pattern of relative statutory tax rates in the United States and other nations during the last decade warrants attention from policymakers.

A third set of proposed tax changes involves incremental reforms to the foreign-source income rules in the current corporation income tax. There is general agreement that the current system of tax rules in the United States is more complex than that in most other nations. The compliance costs of these rules are substantial. The current tax code provisions that discourage the development of joint ventures between U.S.-based firms and foreign partners and the many anti-deferral provisions that raise the tax burdens on U.S. firms relative to foreign firms undertaking the same projects are considered prime candidates for reform.

The corporate tax experts and tax policy scholars who participated in the STEP conference generally agreed on the importance of international tax policy as a factor in corporate decisions with respect to basic research outlays, expenditures on product and process development, and the level of plant and equipment investment. Although the international tax rules are intricate and are not easily explained to those who are not familiar with both the current dynamics of international business and the details of the tax code, they can substantially affect the after-tax return on various investments. These tax rules represent an important part of the tax and regulatory environment in which firms make decisions about the level and composition of R&D spending programs, and they warrant close scrutiny by all policymakers concerned with the level of private-sector spending on technology and capital formation.

# I

INTERNATIONAL TAX POLICY AND
TECHNOLOGY INVESTMENTS

# 1

# The Taxation of Foreign Direct Investment: Operational and Policy Perspectives[1]

JOEL SLEMROD

*University of Michigan*

This chapter has three objectives. First, it provides a brief overview of the U.S. system of taxing the income from foreign direct investment, with particular emphasis on the changes introduced by the last major overhaul of the tax system in the Tax Reform Act of 1986 (TRA86). Second, it reviews the literature assessing the quantitative impact of tax systems on the volume and pattern of foreign direct investment. Finally, the chapter puts international tax rules into a policy perspective by drawing analogies to trade policy.

## U.S. TAXATION OF INCOME FROM FOREIGN DIRECT INVESTMENT

Every country asserts the right to tax the income that is generated within its borders, including the income earned by foreign multinational corporations. Countries differ widely, however, in the tax rates they apply, the definitions of the tax base, and the special incentives they offer for investment. Nevertheless, the first and most important tax burden on foreign direct investment (FDI) is imposed by the government of the "host" country where the investment is located.

Many countries, including the United States, Japan, and the United Kingdom, also assert the right to tax the worldwide income of their residents, including resident corporations. As a general rule, the income of foreign subsidiaries is recognized only on repatriation of earnings through dividends, interest, or royalty

---

[1] Parts of this chapter draw on "The Impact of the Tax Reform Act of 1986 on Foreign Direct Investment to and from the United States" (Slemrod, 1990b); "Comments on Tax Policy and the Activities of Multinational Corporations by James R. Hines, Jr." (Slemrod, 1997); and on "Free Trade Taxation and Protectionist Taxation" (Slemrod, 1995).

payments.[2] To avoid the potentially onerous burden of two layers of taxation, countries that tax on a worldwide basis also offer a credit for income and withholding taxes paid to foreign governments. The total credit available in any given year is usually limited to the home country's tax liability on the foreign-source income, although credits earned in excess of the limitation may often be carried forward or backward to offset excess limitations for other years. Several other countries, including France and the Netherlands, operate a "territorial" system of taxing their resident corporations, under which foreign-source business income is completely exempt from home country taxation.[3]

This would be the end of the story if the geographical location of income were not a matter of dispute. In fact, even if all the information necessary to ascertain the location of income were readily available, the conceptual basis for locating income is controversial (Ault and Bradford, 1990). In reality, corporations have no incentive to reveal fully all the information on which to base a determination of the geographical source of income. For any pattern of real investment decisions, a multinational seeks to shift the apparent source of income out of high-tax countries into low-tax countries. This can be accomplished through, for example, the pricing of intercompany transfers of goods and intangible assets or borrowing through subsidiaries in high-tax countries. Note that this incentive applies regardless of whether the home country operates a territorial or a worldwide system of taxation.

Much of the complexity of the taxation of foreign-source income arises from countries' efforts to defend their revenue base against the fungibility of income tax bases. Complex rules cover standards for acceptable transfer pricing, allocation rules for interest expense and intangibles, and taxing certain types of income on an accrual basis. It is impossible to summarize concisely the various rules that countries employ to determine the location of income. In some countries the statutes are not as important as the outcomes of case-by-case negotiations between representatives of the multinational corporation and government officials. In other cases the source rules are governed by bilateral tax treaties. What is clear, however, is that the *de facto* rules that govern the sourcing of income are at least as important for understanding the effective taxation of foreign direct investment as tax rates, depreciation rules, and tax credits.

The United States operates a worldwide system of taxation. Thus, both the domestic-source income and the foreign-source income of U.S. multinationals are subject to U.S. taxation. For the most part, the income of foreign subsidiaries[4]

---

[2]Unrepatriated earnings may be taxed currently in the case of certain passive or related party income or income earned in "excessive" retention of monies abroad as defined by the so-called subpart F rules of the Internal Revenue Code.

[3]By statute, Canada and Germany have a worldwide system of taxation. However, their tax treaties with the United States provide that repatriated dividends are generally subject to no further tax liability.

[4]The income of foreign branches of U.S. corporations is taxed as accrued. Partly for tax reasons, most foreign activity of U.S. corporations is carried out by subsidiaries rather than branches.

is not taxed as accrued but instead enters the tax base of the U.S. parent upon repatriation of dividends, at which point it is "grossed up" by the average tax rate paid to foreign governments. The grossed-up dividends, minus certain expenses of the multinational allocated to foreign-source income, enter into the taxable income of the parent. Foreign-source income of the parent also includes interest and royalty payments from subsidiaries and certain types of "passive" income on an accrual basis, plus the foreign-source income of foreign branch operations.

In general, income taxes paid by foreign affiliates to foreign governments can be credited against U.S. tax liability. This credit is limited, however, to the U.S. tax liability on the foreign-source income, which is approximately equal to the U.S. statutory corporation tax rate multiplied by the net foreign-source income of the subsidiary. Multinationals whose foreign taxes exceed the limitation on credits are said to be in an *excess credit* position. These excess credits may be carried forward for five years or backward for two years without interest, to be used if and when the parent's potentially creditable taxes fall short of the limitation. If the potentially creditable taxes are less than the limit on credits to be taken in a given year, the corporation is said to be in an *excess limitation* position. Distinguishing excess credit and excess limitation positions is critically important for the financial behavior of a corporation.

## Changed Incentives for Foreign Direct Investment: The Tax Reform Act of 1986

### Outward Investment

The three most significant aspects of TRA86 for outward investment, in order of importance, were as follows: (1) the reduction in the statutory corporate rate from 46 to 34 percent[5] and the resulting increase in the number of firms in an excess credit situation; (2) the change in rules governing the sourcing of income and the allocation of expenses, especially interest expense, between domestic- and foreign-source income; and (3) the tightening of the foreign tax credit limiting the averaging of different types of income.

It is well known that the net effect of the tax system on the incentive to invest depends not only on the statutory rate but also on, among other things, the schedule of depreciation allowances, the rate and scope of investment tax credits, the source of financing, and the rate of inflation. The Tax Reform Act of 1986 eliminated the investment tax credits that previously applied to equipment and machinery and made depreciation allowances somewhat less generous. Both of the steps tended to offset the reduction in the statutory rate of corporate income tax. Most analysts concluded that the net effect of these provisions was to increase

---

[5]The corporate rate has since been increased to 35 percent. To avoid confusion the rest of this chapter refers to a 34 percent, rather than a 35 percent, rate.

slightly the effective corporate-level tax on new domestic investment, an important alternative to FDI.

An analysis of how these same changes affected the effective tax rate on FDI must proceed quite differently because, with certain exceptions, the foreign-source income of foreign subsidiaries enters the parent's tax base only to the extent that dividends are actually, or are deemed to be, repatriated. There is thus no calculation of foreign-source taxable income from which depreciation allowances are deducted and against which investment tax credits can be offset. The tax base to which the corporation statutory tax rate is applied is simply dividends received minus allocable deductions, grossed up by the average rate of foreign taxation. This is calculated using an earnings and profits measure of taxable income, which is not sensitive to legislated changes in the tax depreciation schedules used for domestically located assets,[6] investment credits, and so forth.

Thus, if one ignores the source-of-income rules discussed below, the corporate tax changes of TRA86 reduced the statutory rate from 46 to 34 percent but did not broaden the tax base, resulting in an unambiguous reduction in the tax rate on income from FDI. If the taxes imposed by foreign governments remained unchanged,[7] it follows that the amount of additional taxation imposed by the U.S. upon repatriation either stayed the same or declined. It stayed at zero for multinationals whose average[8] tax rate paid to foreign governments exceeds 46 percent. Any multinational subject to an average tax rate by foreign governments between 34 and 46 percent had formerly been paying taxes upon repatriation but would no longer be liable for any additional taxes under the new rate. For firms paying less than a 34 percent average tax rate to foreign governments, the tax due on repatriation would fall substantially, although not to zero.[9]

Seen from the perspective of 1986, the other important implication of the reduction of the U.S. statutory rate from 46 percent to 34 percent was that a much greater fraction of U.S. multinationals were likely to be in an excess credit

---

[6]The depreciation rules used in the calculation of earnings and profits do, however, change. For example, since 1980 the depreciation rules that apply to property used overseas have been made less generous. These schedules have tax implications because they affect the calculation of tax deemed paid by subsidiaries to foreign governments and the amount of foreign tax credit available for any given amount of dividends remitted.

[7]Since the passage of TRA86, many other countries have enacted tax reforms that share some of the corporate rate-reducing, base-broadening aspects of TRA86. To the extent that TRA86 caused these reforms (or increased their likelihood), the host country effective tax rate was influenced by U.S. tax reform. The analysis that follows holds constant the foreign tax system.

[8]The average tax rate paid to foreign governments is subject to a degree of control by the multinational via its repatriation policy. By repatriating income primarily from high-tax countries, the average tax rate on its foreign-source income is high and less likely to attract additional U.S. tax liability.

[9]Hartman (1985) has argued that regardless of the excess credit status of the U.S. parent, the level of repatriation tax is irrelevant for the incentive to undertake FDI financed by earnings of the foreign subsidiary. This is because the repatriation tax reduces equally both the return to investment and the opportunity cost of investment (reduced dividends). This argument would not apply to the infusion of new equity capital from the parent. See Jun (1989) for a critique of this view.

situation because the average tax paid to foreign governments exceeded 34 percent.[10] For a firm in excess credit status, every additional dollar paid in tax to a foreign government generates a foreign tax credit that cannot be used immediately and has some value to the multinational only if the firm will be in an excess limitation position either in the next five years (the carryforward limit) or had been in an excess limitation position in the previous two years (the carryback limit). Thus, a U.S. multinational in an excess credit position is likely to be much more sensitive to differences in foreign effective tax rates than a firm in an excess limitation situation.[11] This increases the relative attractiveness of investment in a low-rate foreign country such as Ireland, compared to a high-tax country such as Germany.

From a 1997 perspective, however, this increase in excess credit status did not materialize, as Grubert et al. (1996) document. By 1992, about the same fraction of foreign-source income in the general basket was in excess credit as had been the case in 1984. They conclude that the primary reason for this was a decline in average foreign tax rates between 1983 and 1992; it was not attributable in large part to changes in the income or dividend repatriation patterns, or location decisions, of U.S.-based multinational corporations.

A firm in excess credit status can reduce the present value of its tax burden to the extent that it can increase the limit on foreign tax credits. This has increased the importance of rules determining the source, for U.S. tax purposes, of worldwide income. Holding worldwide income constant, if a dollar of income is shifted from domestic source to foreign source, it increases the foreign tax credit limitation by one dollar and allows 34 cents more of foreign taxes to be credited immediately against U.S. tax liability. Only to the extent that foreign governments enforce the same source rules will there be an offsetting increase in foreign tax liability.

One existing source rule that becomes more important applies to production for export. According to current regulations, between 40 and 50 percent of the income from domestic U.S. production of export goods can effectively be allocated to foreign-source income. For a multinational in an excess credit position, this reduces the effective tax rate on domestic investment for export by as much

---

[10]Grubert and Mutti (1987) quote U.S. Treasury Department estimates that the fraction of manufacturing multinationals (weighted by worldwide income) in excess credit would increase from 40 to 69 percent. Goodspeed and Frisch (1989), using updated corporate tax return information, estimate that the fraction of foreign-source income subject to excess credits would rise from 50 to 78 percent, and from 32 to 82 percent in manufacturing. These calculations, however, consider only the change in statutory rate and do not consider changes in the allocation rules or the separate baskets, discussed later. In addition, neither analysis considers changes, perhaps induced by the U.S. reform, in other countries' tax rates. Perhaps most importantly, the analyses do not take into account any behavioral response of the multinationals.

[11]Of course, Hartman's argument implies that for investment financed by retained earnings, only the host country's tax rate matters even for firms in an excess limitation position, so no post-TRA86 increased sensitivity to host country tax rates should be observed.

as half. Thus, if a contemplated FDI is to produce goods for sale outside the United States, the alternative of domestic U.S. production has become relatively tax favored for those firms that have shifted into excess credit status, in spite of the base-broadening aspect of TRA86. This reasoning would not, however, apply to FDI designed to reexport to the United States, because the alternative of domestic production for internal consumption does not benefit from the export source rule.

Interest expenses of the U.S. parent corporation must be allocated to either U.S.-or foreign-source income. The general rule is to allocate on the basis of the book value of assets, so that interest expenses deductible from foreign-source income are equal to total interest payments multiplied by the fraction of world-wide assets represented by assets expected to generate foreign-source income. Although TRA86 did not significantly alter this allocation formula, it did add a "one-taxpayer" rule under which corporations that are members of an affiliated group are consolidated for the purpose of allocating interest expenses between U.S. and foreign sources.[12] In the absence of this rule a multinational could load its debt into a U.S. subsidiary with no foreign-source income and allocate the interest expense entirely to U.S.-source income, thus maximizing foreign-source income and the limitation on foreign tax credits. With the one-taxpayer rule, a fraction of these interest payments has to be allocated to foreign-source income regardless of the legal structure of the multinational.

For multinationals in an excess credit position that are forced to reallocate interest payments, this provision increased the average cost of capital of domestic or foreign investment to the extent debt finance is used. It also increased the marginal cost of foreign investment, because foreign investment increases the amount of interest payments that must be allocated abroad, which decreases foreign-source income and therefore the amount of foreign taxes that are immediately creditable.[13] This provision is obviously most important for multinationals with a high debt-to-capital ratio.

TRA86 also changed the operation of the foreign tax credit by creating separate ("basket") limitations for certain categories of income. Foreign taxes imposed on taxable income in a particular basket can offset only U.S. taxes due on that category of income. There are nine separate baskets, including passive income, high withholding tax interest, and financial services income. In some cases (e.g., passive income), the objective was to prevent fungible income from being earned in low tax rate foreign jurisdictions and thus to increase the amount of available foreign tax credits that could offset taxes paid on other income to foreign governments. In other cases (e.g., high withholding tax interest), the objective was to prevent multinationals (often banks) in an excess limit position

---

[12]The one-taxpayer rule already effectively applied to the allocation of expenses on research and development.

[13]This analysis presumes that the interest allocation rules of foreign governments have not changed.

from paying effectively high withholding taxes (which, due to the excess limit, could be credited immediately against U.S. tax liability) in return for favorable pretax terms of exchange (i.e., higher-than-otherwise pretax interest rates on loans). These objectives share the common thread of limiting the revenue loss to the United States that can arise from manipulation of the foreign tax credit mechanism.

In general, the creation of separate foreign tax credit baskets increases the effective taxation of foreign-source income, because it makes it more difficult in certain cases to credit foreign income taxes against U.S. tax liability. In addition, the baskets can add significant complexity to the typical multinational's compliance procedure, and to this extent the provisions add a hidden tax burden to multinational operation.

*Inward Investment*

Foreign corporations, and U.S. corporations controlled by a foreign corporation, that are engaged in a trade or business in the United States are subject to taxation according to rules that are roughly comparable to those that apply to U.S. corporations. Thus, the reduction of the statutory rate, elimination of the investment tax credit, and changes in depreciation schedules apply directly to foreign subsidiaries. The United States also imposes a "withholding" tax of 30 percent, modified by treaty to a much lower figure for many countries, on payments from corporations within the United States to foreign corporations. These withholding tax rates were not affected by TRA86.

TRA86 did introduce a new branch profits tax, which imposes a 30 percent tax (often reduced by treaty) on the repatriated profits and certain interest payments of a U.S. branch of a foreign corporation. This tax, which affects primarily financial institutions, was designed to equalize the tax treatment of foreign corporations operating through a U.S. branch and those operating through a wholly owned domestic subsidiary.

## IMPACT ON FOREIGN DIRECT INVESTMENT

This is not the place for a comprehensive review of the impact of taxes on foreign direct investment. Fortunately, the interested reader can refer to an up-to-date, careful, and comprehensive review of this topic by Hines (1997). Hines concludes that "taxation exerts a significant effect on the magnitude and location of foreign direct investment," of a magnitude "that is generally consistent with a unit elasticity with respect to after-tax returns." (p. 415)

One aspect that Hines' (1997) paper does not explicitly address is the extent to which the tax impact on foreign investment can be broken down into the impact of the host country's tax system versus that of the home country's tax system. My own reading of the evidence suggests that the potentially significant impact of the former is fairly well established, but the impact of the latter is subject to much more doubt. However, it is the home country tax effect that is critical for understanding how changes in U.S. tax policy affect outbound investment by U.S.-based multinational corporations.

The evidence on this subject is mixed. Slemrod (1990b) fails to uncover any evidence of an effect of the home country tax system on FDI into the United States, in particular whether the home country offers tax credits against tax payments to the United States. Hines (1996), on the other hand, finds strong evidence that the across-state pattern of FDI is consistent with the influence of the home country tax system, in particular that the FDI into high-tax states is more likely to come from home countries that offer tax credits for taxes paid in the United States. Most recently, Grubert and Mutti (1996) analyze tax return data from 500 U.S. multinational corporations to investigate how taxation affects their location decisions. Although they find that host country effective tax rates have a significant effect on both the probability that a location will be chosen and the amount of capital invested there, they find no consistent effect of the parent's excess credit position, which should affect whether it is the tax rate of the host country or the home country that is effective at the margin.

In the face of accumulating evidence of the impact of (at least host country) taxation on FDI, we should be cautious about the policy implications of this research, for two reasons. The first is that the welfare economics of international taxation is very much an unsettled issue (Slemrod, 1995). The second reason is that the estimated response elasticities do not provide adequate information about the structural parameters of the choice problems faced by multinational corporations (MNCs) and, therefore, are not well suited to gauging the impact of particular policy changes.

In other areas of economics we adopt parsimonious enough models so that the estimated parameters map directly into particular structural parameters. For example, under certain assumptions, labor supply elasticities correspond to characteristics of utility functions, and investment demand elasticities inform us about capital-labor substitutability and adjustment cost functions. Yet what does an FDI elasticity inform us about? To answer this question, we need to refer back to the prevailing theory of the nature of a multinational enterprise, coined the "eclectic theory" by Dunning (1985). According to this theory the firm controls certain intangible assets that have a public good aspect to them in that they can be exploited extensively with low marginal cost. The intangible asset is often thought of as information about product or process. To take full (i.e., global) advantage of this intangible the firm could produce its product domestically and export goods embodying the intangible asset, could license the intangible asset to foreign firms and receive a royalty, or could create controlled foreign subsidiaries to produce and distribute the product abroad. As Dunning puts it, FDI by firms of country A in country B is more likely if A's firms (1) possess ownership-specific advantages relative to B's firms in sourcing markets, (2) find it profitable to use these advantages themselves rather than leave them to B's firms, and (3) find it profitable to utilize these ownership-specific advantages in B rather than A. Which choice is taken depends on an array of factors including transportation costs, tariffs, the expropriability of intangibles via licensing arrangements, export subsidies, and the tax rules that apply to foreign direct investment.

Leamer's (1996) terminology is evocative. He contrasts the "mutual fund" model of MNCs, in which the firm allows investors access to foreign equity markets that are otherwise inaccessible, to the idea of an MNC as a kind of "safe-deposit box" that keeps trade secrets from being used by foreign businesses and facilitates the deployment of intangible assets in foreign locations of production. The latter is closer to Dunning's eclectic theory.

Within this conceptual framework it is undoubtedly true that, *ceteris paribus,* a lower effective tax rate on FDI makes it more attractive and thereby should increase its volume. However, what does the measured elasticity of FDI to its after-tax rate of return inform us about? The responsiveness of cross-border capital movements? Not likely, because FDI can be financed largely by local borrowing or local sales of shares, so that increased FDI need not mean increased capital movement. Capital-labor substitutability? Also unlikely, since FDI tells us about who controls a given investment. Certainly the elasticity of who controls the shoe industry in the United States is different from the elasticity of the size of the U.S. shoe industry, regardless of ownership.

The distinction makes a difference not only for how we interpret empirically estimated elasticities but also for the evaluation of policy. Consider the question of optimal tax policy toward inward FDI of a small, open economy. The standard result, discussed in Gordon (1986), is that such a country should, ignoring foreign tax credits offered by the capital-exporting country, impose no distortionary tax on the income earned by capital imports: taxes such as the value-added tax that do not provide a disincentive to investment are allowable. The model generating this standard result conceives of inward FDI as a capital investment, but if the spread of intangibles is involved rather than capital movement, what policy is optimal? If pure profits are at issue, the rate of a tax that is nondistortionary on physical capital investment may matter a great deal.

The real world is messier than Leamer's two-tiered classification suggests because some MNCs do not fit neatly into either of Leamer's categories—they are neither safe-deposit boxes nor mutual funds. Consider the Cook Island corporations set up to accept the funds of New Zealand residents to be invested back into New Zealand—the so-called Cook Island runaround. Many such firms are simply conduits designed to suck in taxable profits from other relatively high-tax jurisdictions, and as such are tax shell games. There are tax haven countries that are, for a fee, in the business of facilitating MNC tax avoidance. The presence of tax havens and the opportunities for avoidance and evasion they provide are a key reason that the tax regimes governing MNCs are so complex. They make a nod toward efficient allocation of resources by offering schemes to avoid punitive double taxation, but often they are largely antitax avoidance devices.

Recognizing the opportunities for income shifting puts a new slant on what is appropriate policy. Consider the example of a country that decides to stimulate domestic investment by lowering its effective tax rate. It has two choices. One is to keep its current statutory corporate tax rate at 35 percent and introduce a generous investment tax credit. The other is to lower the statutory rate to 25 percent, or even to 10 percent, as Ireland has done. Presume that both policies provide equal Hall-Jorgenson-King-Fullerton effective tax rates. Will the two policies have the same impact on domestic investment? The answer is no, because only the low statutory rate regime has the attraction that once operations are located in the country, taxable income can be shifted in from other high-tax locations to lower the MNC's worldwide tax burden. To capture this distinction requires the construction of what in Grubert and Slemrod (forthcoming) is referred to as an "income-shifting-adjusted cost of capital," or ISACC. The ISACC measures the true cost of capital for real investment because it accounts for the possibility that real investment facilitates income shifting.[14]

The next generation of empirical studies must be based on structural theoretical models that lay out both the "real" choices involved, such as the location of real investment or research and development operations, and the array of other choices an MNC faces, including financing, income shifting opportunities, and in some contexts, retiming opportunities. The interaction among these choices will certainly be critical. For example, are avoidance opportunities independent of real choices, or are they facilitated by some real choices? In at least some contexts, the latter is certainly true. Grubert and Slemrod (forthcoming) find that U.S. real investment in Puerto Rico is driven primarily by the income shifting opportunities Puerto Rican operations afford, as evidenced by the predominance of high-margin production located there.

The first generation of empirical research on MNCs has established conclusively that the answer to the question, Do Taxes Matter? is yes. A new generation of research, based on structural models of the joint decisions regarding real decision and tax avoidance is required to answer the next question, How do taxes matter? This question presents a fascinating intellectual challenge of integrating models of the nature of the multinational enterprise and opportunities for tax avoidance into normative models of tax policy. It is an important challenge because the international tax system is gaining prominence as economies integrate, MNCs expand, and traditional barriers to trade fall.

---

[14] I argue in Slemrod (1994) that this point applies much more broadly than to MNC investment. For example, if the increased income from more labor supply facilitates more tax avoidance, then its true marginal tax rate lies below the statutory marginal tax rate. In this case, estimated labor supply elasticities do not directly reveal information about utility functions but instead reveal a mixture of information about utility functions and the tax avoidance technology.

## PUTTING INTERNATIONAL TAX RULES
## INTO POLICY PERSPECTIVE

It is clear that we are a long way from having a definitive understanding of how taxation affects foreign direct investment. It is also clear that the formulation of international tax policy cannot be postponed until that understanding is acquired. Policy formulation is often driven by short-run revenue considerations, rather than on the basis of a consistent set of underlying principles or objectives. When objectives are articulated, they are often ill-defined, as in the case of ensuring "international competitiveness."

In the remainder of this chapter I attempt to seek new insight and a new language for international tax policy by recasting it in parallel with the theory of international trade. The potential gains from such an exercise are twofold. First, although international trade theory has been applied principally to policy instruments such as tariffs, quotas, and dumping, tax policy can have at least as large an effect on the flow of goods across countries, the location of productive activity, and the gains from trade as these trade policy instruments. Thus, it is an important object of study in its own right. Second, certain propositions about trade—the benefits of free trade and the costs of protectionism, for example—have a long history and are reasonably noncontroversial among economists. Drawing on this reasoning can clarify the murky issues involved in international taxation.

The potential disadvantage of this comparison is that although the preference toward free trade is well established among economists, it is not well established elsewhere. On the contrary, the debate over trade policy continues, with the economist's view sometimes prevailing and sometimes not prevailing. The risk is that the prejudices and misconceptions regarding trade policy will simply be attached to the issues of international tax policy, thereby blurring issues rather than sharpening them. Yet this is not necessarily a problem, because implicitly it is already happening. To make the linkage explicit should be an advance.

In what follows I purposely do not use the standard catch phrases of international tax policy, such as capital export neutrality, capital import neutrality, and national neutrality. Nevertheless, many of the familiar arguments reappear here in somewhat different guises. I begin by restating the classic case for free trade; the remainder of the chapter draws out its implications for income tax policy in a global economy.

### The Case for Free Trade

The case for free trade is that the gains from trade, and therefore national income, are maximized when domestic consumers and producers face world prices that are undistorted by import tariffs, export subsidies, and the like. Consumers are made better off by the opportunity to exchange at world prices domestically produced goods for goods that can be obtained from abroad. The benefit from this exchange of goods will be maximized if domestic producers produce the goods and services that have the greatest possible value on world markets. They will do this in their own interest if they are free to trade at world prices. Not all members of a society will be better off from a move toward free trade, but as national income increases, all citizens could be made better off with a suitable redistributive policy.

According to this reasoning, free trade practiced by all countries will maximize world income. More importantly, a free trade policy adopted unilaterally will maximize the adopting country's national income, regardless of the trade policies of other countries. Even if a trading partner is subsidizing its exports, the importing country is better off not to respond by shielding its residents from world prices. As Krugman and Obstfeld put it, the appropriate response is to send the subsidizing country a "note of thanks" for offering its goods at bargain prices (1991, p. 112). As to countering a trading partner's tariffs with tariffs of one's own, Joan Robinson remarked that "it would be just as sensible to drop rocks into our harbors because other nations have rocky coasts"(1947, p. 192). Economists' difficulty in communicating these ideas to noneconomists has stimulated their invention of vivid metaphors.

The classic case for free trade depends on a number of assumptions about how the economy operates. In the absence of these assumptions, a case for trade policy intervention can be made. Briefly these are the principal arguments:

1. If a country has monopoly or monopsony power with regard to a commodity, a tariff or subsidy can enable the country to profit from it. In the case of monopoly, the country ought to tax the export of the commodity to drive up its world price; in the case of monopsony, it ought to impose a tariff on imports to drive down the price it pays for the good.

2. If the domestic economy is distorted, trade intervention could offset the distortion and thereby increase national income. The distortion could be due to domestic tax policy, the lack of perfect capital markets for "infant" industries, or some other practice. In general, it is better to eliminate the distortion than to counteract it with trade policy because trade intervention introduces new distortions even if it reduces others. Deardorff and Stern compare trade policy to "acupuncture with a fork; no matter how carefully you insert one prong, the other is likely to do damage" (1987, p. 39).

3. In the presence of oligopolistic markets, judicious policy can shift some of the pure profits from foreign firms to domestic firms. If domestic firms are owned by domestic residents, this can increase national income. Such a policy works only under rather restrictive conditions, which are difficult to identify empirically, regarding the nature of the oligopolistic market. For this reason, designing a successful policy of selective intervention is impractical.

4. Countervailing duties may be strategically useful as a means of discouraging other countries from using opportunistic trade policies.

There are also noneconomic arguments for trade intervention, such as foreign policy or national security concerns, and domestic considerations, but I will not address them here.

With the exception of distortion-offsetting arguments, note that the rationales for trade intervention are all beggar-thy-neighbor policies. To the extent that they increase national income, they do so at the expense of income in the rest of the world. Moreover, the decline in income elsewhere will exceed the gain in domestic national income, so from a global perspective these policies are wasteful. For this reason, a multilateral agreement to eliminate such practices can potentially increase each participating country's national income, given the possibility of transfers across countries.

The classical case for free trade advises any country to adopt free trade unilaterally, regardless of what goes on elsewhere. Most free traders do not, however, advocate unilateral free trade without qualification. Instead they support multilateral commercial policy agreements such as the General Agreement on Tariffs and Trade or World Trade Organization and, more recently, regional free trade arrangements such as the North American Free Trade Agreement. Often they support unilateral strategic use of commercial policies, such as countervailing duties and antidumping actions, to induce other countries to adopt free trade policies. Other countries' movement toward free trade will in general, although not in every instance, benefit one's own country, so it is worthwhile to encourage these policies. In addition, a unilateral free trade stance is less viable politically in the face of commercial policy interventions by foreign governments unless it is accompanied by "concessions" made by other countries.

In summary, the trade policy prescriptions are (1) unilateral free trade as a rule of thumb, (2) toleration of strategic use of protectionist measures as a device to eliminate trade barriers elsewhere, and (3) support of multilateral agreements to lower trade barriers.

## Meaning of Free Trade Taxation

What international tax policies do these prescriptions suggest? To answer this question, I must define the concept of free trade taxation, first in the global context and then in the unilateral context.

First, recall that the orthodox free trade position is that there should be no tariffs or nontariff trade restrictions at all. This simple stance is obviously not applicable directly to tax policy for the simple reason that the U.S. federal tax system must raise well over $1 trillion annually. There must be tax revenue, and lots of it, and all taxes other than so-called lump-sum taxes distort some margin of choice, such as the work-leisure choice, the consumption-saving choice, or the invest-or-not choice and therefore are the source of inefficiencies.

How to design the *minimally* distorting tax system, subject to the other goals of the tax system such as equity and simplicity, has preoccupied public finance economists for more than half a century. Unfortunately, no consensus has arisen on simple rules for achieving this goal. Diamond and Mirrlees (1971) advanced one proposition, however, with far-reaching implications. It states that given certain strong conditions, a tax system should, whatever other distortions it introduces, preserve "production efficiency." The required conditions are that pure profits either do not exist or can be fully taxed away and that a broad set of fiscal instruments can be utilized. Production efficiency is achieved when all firms face the same input prices, including the same cost of capital, and all firms face the same price of output. When this is violated, it would be possible, by reallocating production among firms, to increase the value of output for the same amount of inputs. In other words, failure to achieve production efficiency implies that the economy is operating with avoidable waste.

In a completely closed economy, production efficiency is compatible with either consumption taxes or a pure income tax, where "pure" implies a Haig-Simons comprehensive definition of income, including integration of the corporate and personal income tax systems. Under a pure income tax the cost of capital to firms will exceed the rate of return received by savers, but it will be equal for all firms, preserving production efficiency. Under a consumption tax the cost of capital is equal for all firms and is equal to the rate of return for savers.

The proposition that an optimal tax system will achieve production efficiency obviously does not hold in the world economy of 1997. Thus, in principle there are instances in which this desideratum ought to be abandoned, although it is exceedingly difficult to describe analytically what these cases look like. In the following section I use some aspects of production efficiency to establish a conceptual standard for free trade in capital and to assess under what conditions an income tax-based system can achieve this standard.

*Global Optimality*

From a global perspective, production efficiency is achieved and worldwide income is maximized only if all investments face the same risk-adjusted "hurdle rate," or pretax required rate of return, regardless of where the real investment is located, the nationality of the investing firm's headquarters, or the citizenship of the capital owner. This condition ensures that investments with lower pretax (i.e., social) rates do not, for tax reasons, get made while investments with higher pretax returns stay on the shelf. This is the standard for free trade in capital, including both tangible and intangible capital.

Consider a world in which each national economy is completely closed off from all others. In this case the hurdle rate in each country will be determined by the interaction among domestic residents' propensity to save, domestic investment opportunities, and tax and other government policies that affect the rate of return. There is no reason to expect the hurdle rate to be equal across countries and therefore no reason for global production efficiency to be satisfied. It is conceivable that investments that could earn 15 percent in one country will not go forward, while at the same time investments located in another country yielding 8 percent will be undertaken.

One potential benefit of opening up these closed economies is the amelioration of production inefficiency. Some of this will be accomplished if borders are opened only to trade in goods and services, but not to financial or investment flows, via the "factor price equalization" mechanism familiar to international trade economists. Capital-intensive goods will be relatively costly to produce in countries with a relatively high cost of capital and will tend to be imported rather than produced domestically, whereas labor- or land-intensive goods will tend to be produced domestically and exported. The sectoral shift of production will reduce the demand for capital in these countries, pushing down the cost of capital. The same mechanism in reverse will increase the cost of capital in countries that, in the absence of trade, had a relatively low cost of capital and marginal return to investment.

Trade in goods and services is unlikely, by itself, to eliminate differences in the return to investment because of different technologies of production, specialization of production, and the existence of natural barriers and man-made barriers to trade flows. Thus, even with international trade in goods and services, cross-country differences in pretax required rates of return are likely to persist. The free international flow of capital can, depending on its tax treatment, alleviate this production inefficiency.

## What Tax Structures Are Consistent with Global Production Efficiency?

What pattern of tax rates and systems, including the corporate, personal, and withholding tax rates and the system of double taxation relief, will ensure that free trade in capital is achieved? The answer to this question depends on, among other things, what assumptions are made about the extent of capital and labor mobility. Unless otherwise stated, I presume perfect capital mobility—all investments available to all investors on equal terms, tax rules aside—and no labor mobility. These are stylized assumptions meant to capture the current reality that capital is much more mobile across national boundaries than is labor.

One pattern that works is a pure residence-based tax system. Under this system, residents of each country are taxed on all their capital income, perhaps with a progressive rate structure, regardless of where the physical investment is located or what process of intermediation it passes through. This could be achieved either if source countries forgo any taxation of nonresidents' earnings within the country or if all countries tax the worldwide income of their residents upon accrual and offset source countries' taxes by offering an unlimited foreign tax credit. Under the first method, a country that levies an integrated corporation income tax must rebate any taxes collected from foreign owners. For example, a wholly foreign-owned domestic corporation would owe to the host country no corporation tax and certainly no withholding taxes. No foreign tax credit system would be needed for any country since no government collects taxes from foreigners in the first place.

Under the second method, all corporate income tax systems would have to be integrated, so that the corporate tax acts essentially as a withholding tax for the personal tax system. Integration benefits would have to be granted to foreign shareholders, coordinated by the investor's home country so that the total rate of tax is no different for foreign and domestic investments. Countries' corporate tax rates need not be identical for production efficiency to occur. For any given set of personal tax systems, a high corporate rate would be offset by higher imputation credits granted at the personal level to shareholders in the affected corporations.

It is important to note that the concept of residency used above refers to individuals, not to the legal or tax residence of corporations. A residence-based tax of this type would have to look through the corporate entity to the individual shareholders, so that the total tax burden on any given shareholder would not depend on the rate of source-based tax that is levied in any jurisdiction or on the legal residency of corporations whose shares are owned. Under such a system, higher taxes paid by a corporation, given constant worldwide rates of personal tax, would be accompanied by lower taxes payable by the shareholders. The apparent corporate tax penalty is exactly offset by a lower cost of capital to the firm.

For production efficiency, it is not necessary that all countries levy the *same* rate of tax on their residents. Nor is it required that any country levy the same rate on all of its citizens. In the presence of these differences, the pretax hurdle rate would be the same in all locations, but the after-tax rate of return earned by any individual saver would depend inversely on the rate of tax levied by his or her home government.

Current international tax arrangements are a long way from this pure residence-based system because of concerns over national sovereignty and certain inescapable administrative and compliance concerns. No country has seen fit to refrain from taxing the excellent tax "handle" afforded by domestically located, but foreign-owned, capital. Furthermore, as long as some countries continue to tax on a worldwide basis, lowering source-based tax often merely transfers revenue from the host country to the home country treasury. Second, there is concern that if foreign-owned capital were exempt from taxation, domestic residents would be able to set up foreign corporations and thereby avoid taxation. Finally, and related to the foregoing concerns, it is much more difficult for a country to monitor and collect tax revenue from tax bases located outside the country. For this reason, many countries do not even subject foreign-source income to taxation; many of those that do so are not very successful in collecting it.

Taking account of the administrative and compliance costs of taxation implies that a pure residence-based tax is not optimal. It is certainly not close to what we observe today. What about the other extreme alternative, a pure source-based tax? Under this system, each country taxes all income generated within its borders at the same rate, regardless of who owns the assets, and forgoes any taxation on the foreign-source income of its citizens. This would involve a flat-rate business tax, no additional personal income tax on corporate income, and no withholding taxes.

To summarize what international tax systems are consistent with free trade in capital, defined as equal hurdle rates for all investments, either a pure residence-based or a pure source-based system with equal tax rates in all countries is consistent with production efficiency. However, administrative and compliance considerations suggest that the residence-based system is impractical, and there is no reason to expect harmonization of source-based tax rates. Hybrid systems with elements of both source-based and residence-based taxation can also be consistent with equal hurdle rates.

The current system certainly does not replicate exactly any of the structures that would be consistent with free trade, just as worldwide tariff and other commercial policies are not consistent with complete free trade in goods and services. This implies that alternate policies could increase world income.

## Unilateral Free Trade Taxation

Let me now put aside the meaning of free trade taxation in a global context and return to appropriate unilateral tax policy. By analogy to trade policy, the first prescription is that as a rule of thumb, unilateral free trade taxation should be pursued. Yet what exactly does unilateral free trade mean in the context of capital income taxes? Although I focus on outbound foreign investment, there should be a few words about efficient taxation of inbound investment. As mentioned earlier, it is a well-known result in optimal taxation (see, e.g., Gordon, 1986) that under certain conditions, a small open economy should impose no investment-reducing tax on inbound investment. The conditions include abstracting from administrative and compliance concerns. Note also that certain taxes on inbound investment may not be investment reducing if the capital-exporting country offers a foreign tax credit.

As discussed above, this theorem has not prevented source-based taxation of capital income from being the international norm, one that is likely to persist. This raises the question of the appropriate tax treatment of outbound foreign investment in a world where source-based taxation is the norm. Because the answer will be counterintuitive to some, let me pursue the analogy with trade policy regarding goods and services. If a foreign country levies import duties, what is the appropriate response of the exporting country? The unilateral free trade response is to allow such goods to leave the country at the world price and let the importing country's domestic price be higher than the world price because of the import duty. It is not appropriate to levy an export subsidy high enough to offset the import tariff.

The analogy to the taxation of cross-border flows of income from investment is as follows. If the country in which the investment is located levies a tax, the country in which the investor is resident should offer no credit for these taxes. Furthermore, if a country wishes to levy an income tax on its residents, the base for such a tax should be income net of taxes levied by the source country (this argument was made in Richman, 1963). It is as if the source country is levying a tax on imports of capital. The capital-exporting country, in its own interest, ought not to offset it with an export subsidy.

In practice, no country, and certainly not the United States, follows this policy. Instead all capital-exporting countries offer some form of offset to taxes imposed by the source country, either in the form of a limited tax credit for foreign taxes paid or by exempting foreign-source income from the taxation that is applied to domestic-source income. However, as discussed above, some countries with imputation systems of integration can effectively impose an additional level of taxes on foreign direct investment.

The U.S. policy of providing foreign tax credits has been characterized as "mercantilist" by Schmidt (1975) because it favors foreign investment at the expense of the national interest. This claim is correct from a unilateral perspective because it is in the interest of one country to ensure that at the margin, the return to the country of all investments be equal, and the return to the country includes taxes paid to the country and not taxes paid to the host country. Thus, full taxation of foreign investment income with deductibility of foreign taxes paid is unilaterally appropriate but not consistent with global free trade in the presence of ubiquitous source-based taxes. Is it appropriate to characterize full taxation with deductibility as beggar-thy-neighbor behavior? In a sense it is, because the loss from this policy to the host country due to lost investment would exceed the gain to the capital-exporting nation. This usage of the term is somewhat strained, though, as the trade analogy makes clear: if all importing countries impose a tariff on a particular good, then it is beggar-thy-neighbor for an exporting country *not* to impose an export subsidy.

In practice, all nations forgo the unilaterally optimal but beggar-thy-neighbor policy and, in so doing, avoid one route to double taxation of foreign investment that would be inimical to global free trade. It is as if, faced with tariffs imposed by all nations importing a certain good, all the exporting nations imposed exactly offsetting export subsidies. This would eliminate any trade distortions and thus be optimal from a global perspective, but it would not be in the exporting countries' interest because it would essentially be a transfer payment to a foreign government. Thus, it is inevitable that the division of revenues becomes an important and contentious element of the current international tax regime. Bilateral tax treaties generally feature a reciprocity clause, requiring equal withholding levies for capital flows in both directions. This is designed to maintain an equitable distribution of tax revenues in the presence of two-way capital flows. Whether it in fact achieves this goal depends also on the corporate tax rates and the details of the integration systems in placc (Ault, 1992).

Thus, a basic feature of U.S. taxation of foreign-source income, the alleviation of double taxation, cannot be defended on the ground of unilateral free trade but must be viewed as part of a system that could be consistent with global free trade. However, other aspects of international tax policy can be made consistent with unilateral free trade, in the sense of avoiding beggar-thy-neighbor policies. For example, because the U.S. domestic saving and investment is large relative to world markets, it likely has some monopoly power, namely, the ability to affect world interest rates. If the United States is a net capital exporter it can take advantage of its power by taxing capital exports, thus driving up the rate of return on its net exports. If it is a net capital importer, it should tax capital imports, thus driving down the rate of return it must pay on such imports. The spirit of unilateral free trade dictates that these opportunities not be exploited.

The prescriptions for free trade include the possible use of strategic policies directed at countries that do not themselves play by the rules of global free trade. Are there any useful analogies of this idea to international tax policy? Can one identify tax actions that are protectionist in nature and could justify "countervailing" tax action?

Discrimination against foreign-owned firms would probably qualify. However, most developed countries pledge nondiscrimination of company taxation through the existing network of bilateral tax treaties. A standard feature of these treaties is a clause stipulating that tax treatment of a domestic company will not depend on whether the company is domestic or foreign owned.

Thus, two of the fundamental features of the international tax structure—avoidance of double taxation and nondiscrimination—are broadly consistent with, but by no means ensure, global free trade. Continued adherence to these principles is clearly desirable, but leaves many aspects of a country's international tax regime unspecified. It also leaves unclear what criterion ought to be used to evaluate these aspects. Should the criterion be unilateral national income maximization, with the presumption that adherence to double taxation relief and nondiscrimination fulfills the country's obligations to free trade? Alternatively, should the United States seek to extend the range of policies that if adopted multilaterally, can, by enhancing free trade in capital, potentially lead to increased national income at home and abroad? This is a critical question underlying all policy analysis of international tax policy, but it is usually left implicit.

## Aspects of Tax Policy:  Free Trade or Protectionist?

*Border Protectionism and Ownership Protectionism*

One important difference between trade policy and tax policy is that whereas trade policy operates at the border and is blind to corporate residency, tax policy can operate at the margin of corporate residency. For example, U.S. tariffs are imposed on all imported products, regardless of whether the good is produced abroad by a foreign-owned company or an affiliate of a U.S.-owned company. Domestically produced goods are not subject to tariffs and benefit or suffer, if the imported goods are inputs, from the higher domestic prices caused by tariffs, regardless of whether the producer is U.S. or foreign owned. Thus, trade policy raises the issue of what might be called "border protectionism."

Income taxation, because it can impose differential taxation depending on corporate residence, may also involve another kind of protectionism that I term "ownership protectionism," although this is something of a misnomer to the extent of international diversification of share ownership. Whether it does or does not depends on the structure of the income tax in place. If, for example, all countries scrupulously practiced nondiscrimination of business enterprises, levied no withholding taxes, and operated territorial systems of taxation, any two corporations with the same real operations and results spread over the world would pay the same total tax, regardless of the residency of the parent corporations and even in the face of varying tax rates across countries. A French company and a U.S. company would pay the same total tax if both companies operated exclusively in the United States, exclusively in France, exclusively in Singapore, or in some combination of these and/or other countries.

Differences can arise, though, because the United States taxes its resident multinationals on a worldwide basis and France taxes on a territorial basis. In this case there is a potential tax penalty placed on a U.S. multinational versus a French multinational that depends on the locational pattern of activity. There would be no substantial difference if the two multinationals operated exclusively in countries of similar tax rates such as France and the United States. The difference arises to the extent that operations are located in a low-tax country. The U.S. parent company, but not the French parent, could be subject to a residual tax upon repatriation of income from its affiliate in the low-tax country. The apparent difference is also mitigated if the U.S. multinational operates not only in low-tax countries but also in foreign countries with average tax rates that exceed the U.S. average rate. In this case the U.S. system allows repatriated income from a low-tax country such as Ireland to be "mixed" with repatriated income from a high-tax country such as Germany, with the result that no net tax need be paid to the U.S. government.

From the standpoint of global efficiency, there is no reason that the total corporate plus individual tax burden on the income of a multinational enterprise should depend on the parent company's country of incorporation. It is no more efficient than, in a domestic context, taxing corporations with names beginning with the letters A through K at one rate, while taxing at a higher rate those with names beginning with L through Z—and not allowing name changes. If enacted, Lollapollooza Corporation could not compete with Kennebunkport Corporation if they produced exactly the same products. If they produced slightly different products, Lollapollooza might survive, but on a smaller scale and with a diminished variety of output. As Frisch (1990) has argued, one efficiency cost of this discrimination could be a reduced variety of products available to the world market.

Whether higher corporate taxes translate into higher total taxes depends on the tax system in place. This would not occur if all countries adopted a pure residence-based tax, where residence refers to the residence of individuals and not corporations. Corporations subject to more tax would necessarily have shareholders who had a lower personal tax burden, so their cost of capital would be low enough to offset the higher corporation tax payments. Under the current international system of taxation, which is not a pure residence-based system and not perfectly integrated, this offset will not occur.

Some have claimed that a tax penalty on U.S. resident multinational enterprises would be especially harmful to the U.S. national interest. One argument is that legal residence generally is associated with "headquarters" activities, such as research and development, that are especially beneficial to U.S. economic performance. If these benefits to the country cannot be captured by the firms themselves, there is an economic argument for subsidizing, and certainly not penalizing, such "externality"-producing activities. A relatively high tax rate on the worldwide activities of U.S.-based multinationals would, over the long run, divert economic activity to other multinationals, reducing the amount of headquarters activities carried out in this country.

This argument ignores the availability of alternative policies that are better targeted to address the externalities issue. Any specific activities, associated with the headquarters of multinational enterprises or not, that produce positive externalities should be subsidized and, for the most part, already are. Research and development expenditures, for example, may be expensed rather than amortized for tax purposes and furthermore are eligible for an incremental tax credit. It may be that the current effective rate of subsidy is too low, but this argues for raising it. Yet the rate of tax on all U.S.-headquartered multinational enterprises, regardless of their externality-producing activities, is too blunt an instrument for this purpose.

Another line of argument is based on the empirical fact that U.S. companies tend to be owned primarily by U.S. citizens, whereas foreign companies tend to be owned by foreigners. In this circumstance it would be in the national interest to have policies that shift profits from foreign to U.S. companies. In oligopolistic markets, tax breaks can work just as well as export subsidies in shifting profits toward domestic firms. However, as Levinsohn and Slemrod (1993) show, in the simplest case this profit shifting is best achieved by subsidizing the output of domestic firms, not by distinguishing between domestically located and foreign-located production and allowing foreign taxes as a deduction. There may, though, be a case for favoring foreign operations if some sectors are perfectly competitive and some are oligopolistic and if trade policy, but not tax policy, can be sector specific. In this case a tariff may have to be used, and location nonneutrality tolerated, so as to target the subsidy to the oligopolistic industries. In this case the targeting advantage of trade policy over tax policy overrides the production inefficiency caused by the tariff.

### Income Shifting and Tax Havens

Another important difference between tariff policy and tax policy is that the basis for duties is the value of transaction, whereas the basis for income tax policy is a measure of income. Income is a considerably more slippery concept to define, and the *location* of the income of an integrated global enterprise is a conceptual nightmare. Ault and Bradford (1990) have gone so far as to argue that it is not meaningful.

Given differences in tax rates across countries and the fact that no country has a pure residence-based system of taxing corporations, there are incentives to take advantage of the difficulty of locating income to reduce an enterprise's worldwide tax burden. A multinational operating in two countries in which the marginal tax rate on a dollar of income is different would, ceteris paribus, prefer to shift income from the high-tax country to the low-tax country. Such shifting can be accomplished by the judicious setting of prices of transactions between corporate affiliates or by judicious international financial policy such as borrowing in high-tax countries.

In holding the location of real activity constant, a country gains when a dollar of taxable income is shifted into it, while the country from which it is shifted loses. The world is currently populated by a set of countries, known loosely as tax havens, that set low marginal tax rates and look the other way—or even encourage—the inward shifting of taxable income. To stanch the outward flow of taxable income, countries that have relatively high tax rates must establish an enforcement structure to monitor transfer pricing, earnings stripping, and other methods of income shifting.

Tax havens can be classified into two types. In one type, the country levies a very low tax rate on the income from manufacturing operations located in its jurisdiction. In the second type, the country offers a low tax on the income of corporations whose legal domicile is that country. One motivation behind becoming the first type of tax haven is to attract real investment and economic activity into the country. This is not a primary motivation behind the second kind of tax haven. In that case the country is essentially offering its services, for a fee, to individuals and corporations pursuing tax avoidance and evasion.

Even the first type of tax haven opportunistically gains from income shifting. Consider the example of Ireland, which offers a preferential tax rate of 10 percent on the income reported due from manufacturing operations in that country. Having established an affiliate in Ireland, a multinational enterprise has the incentive to shift taxable profits to that country from higher-tax countries. Thus, it is no coincidence that such countries implement a low marginal effective tax rate on investment via a low statutory tax rate strategy as opposed to a strategy of a high statutory rate combined with generous investment tax credits and/or depreciation allowances. Although any particular low marginal effective tax rate can be obtained with the latter strategy, it would not make the country a magnet for income shifting, only for real activity.

Local content rules are a useful analogy to tax havens in the domain of international trade. Imagine that the United States imposes quantity restrictions on the import of steel from Japan and Korea. To enforce such restrictions, there must be a way to identify imports from an unrestricted country, such as Mexico, as having originated in Mexico rather than in Japan or Korea. This is usually accomplished by attempting to measure the "local content" of the imports from Mexico and requiring it to be above a prespecified level to be imported without restriction. These rules are similar to the anti-treaty shopping provisions of income tax treaties, which seek to limit the rerouting of income through tax havens to minimize tax payments. A country that for some compensation, collaborates with the restricted countries to evade the U.S. local content rules is acting similarly to a tax haven. I refer to this behavior as "predatory tax protectionism." It is predatory because it is clearly a zero-sum or a negative-sum game in which the tax haven's gains are offset by losses to the rest of the world.

From a global perspective, the presence of tax havens is costly for at least two reasons. First, there are substantial resource costs expended by the tax collection agencies of the rest of the world to minimize inappropriate income shifting and substantial resources costs expended by the multinationals themselves to accomplish such shifting. Second, there are distortions in the kind of real activity that the first type of tax haven attracts (i.e., high-margin production such as pharmaceuticals and electronics that facilitate income shifting). Absent income shifting considerations, there is no economic reason why such activities should be located in Ireland or Puerto Rico, which can offer income shifting advantages to U.S. corporations.

I have argued elsewhere (Slemrod, 1988) that the costs due to tax havens and income shifting are appropriately dealt with via a multilateral agreement restricting statutory corporate tax rates to a small band and imposing sanctions on countries that choose not to comply. Countries would be permitted to be magnets for real investment, but they would have to do so by offering investment tax credits rather than low statutory tax rates. A minimum statutory corporate tax rate is the approach suggested as a first step toward more corporate tax harmonization by the Ruding committee, the experts' committee of the European Commission charged with recommending what, if any, tax harmonization should be adopted in concert with the 1992 curtailment of barriers to free trade in goods and services; this suggestion was not, however, embraced by the European Community.

On a unilateral basis, it is imperative that the U.S. international tax system be designed to counteract predatory tax protectionism. It is clear that U.S. rules in this regard impose large costs on multinationals operating here (see Blumenthal and Slemrod, 1995), but it is also evident that the potential stakes involved in income shifting are large (Harris et al., 1993). In a domestic context it does not generally make economic sense to push tax enforcement until the point where, at the margin, revenue gained equals cost, because the revenue gained does not represent a benefit to the country but instead is a transfer of resources. In the context of international income shifting, revenue gained does represent a benefit to the country, although not to the world as a whole, because it comes at the expense of a foreign treasury. Thus, it does make sense from a unilateral perspective to push enforcement much harder in an income shifting context than in a domestic context. From a global perspective, as suggested above, there will be an inefficiently large expenditure on this kind of enforcement.

### Worldwide or Territorial System?

Because it involves most of the issues discussed above, let me address the choice between taxing worldwide income, with a limited foreign tax credit, and taxing only income earned within the United States. To be precise, the territorial alternative I consider would tax passive or portfolio income on a worldwide basis but tax active business income on a territorial basis.

Because either system affords relief from double taxation, either is generally consistent with free trade. However, a territorial system allows and, relative to a worldwide system, encourages host countries to attract capital investment by offering a low marginal effective tax rate. This is inimical to free trade because it implies that the hurdle rate will be lower in these countries than elsewhere. It allows lower rates because there is no residual tax imposed by the U.S. government. It encourages low rates because high rates are less likely to be offset by credits from the home country government once the United States gets out of the business of offering foreign tax credits. Only Japan and the United Kingdom will remain, and these countries have tax sparing treaties with many developing countries essentially exempting foreign-source income earned in the treaty partners' countries from residual taxation by the home country.

How does the choice look from a unilateral perspective? First of all, the territorial system is simpler to administer and comply with than the worldwide system, so a switch will in the long run save on collection costs. However, as Tillinghast (1991) has noted, an exemption system would still be complex both because passive and active income would have to be distinguished and because a territorial system would increase the potential gains from income shifting and therefore put pressure on the transfer pricing rules and other enforcement tools.

Another important criterion is whether a worldwide system of taxation offers a better defense against predatory tax protectionism in the form of tax havens. Does the potential residual tax imposed upon either accrual or repatriation provide an important backstop to our attempt to tax domestic-source income in the same way that the corporation tax can be justified as a backstop to the objective of taxing capital and labor income in general? This important question remains open. In this regard it would be worthwhile to compare the success of countries such as France and the Netherlands that operate territorial systems.

How do the two systems stack up with regard to ownership protectionism? There is no compelling reason for the U.S. government either to penalize or to subsidize U.S.-parented multinational enterprises versus those of other countries. Under the current system there is a relative tax penalty to U.S. multinationals whose foreign operations are predominantly in low-tax countries; the United States will impose a residual tax on repatriated earnings, a tax not owed by non-U.S. multinationals.

Note, however, that a careful recent study (Grubert and Mutti, 1993) concludes that the tax shortfall from switching to an exemption system would be small, $0.2 billion compared to $97.9 billion of foreign-source income. This is because many of the U.S. multinationals that operate in low-tax countries also operate in high-tax countries and thereby can set their repatriation strategy to avoid any residual tax to the U.S. government. It is also because some U.S. multinationals now repatriate a mix of high-taxed dividends with low-taxed royalty and interest income to avoid substantial residual tax. Under an exemption system, the dividend income would be exempt, but the royalty income would still face worldwide taxation subject to a foreign tax credit.

These revenue estimates suggest that when all U.S. multinationals are considered as a group, whatever ownership tax penalty currently exists is small and would not be altered significantly by the change to a territorial system. A cautionary note about the revenue estimates is in order, though, because they depend critically on an assumption of minimal behavioral response to the change in tax regime. This is unlikely however. For example, repatriations now labeled as royalties could be reclassified as dividends, thus avoiding U.S. tax. The extent of this kind of "relabeling elasticity" is difficult to forecast accurately.

## CONCLUSIONS

Compatibility with free trade is not the only standard against which to judge an international tax system. Its implications for equity, within and across countries and its consistency with domestic tax regimes are two other important criteria. Nevertheless, as national economies become more integrated and as barriers to trade in goods and services fall, the importance of international taxation for the efficient functioning of capital markets will become a central concern.

Free trade in capital is achieved only if the hurdle rate for investment is equal regardless of the location of the real activity, the nationality of the corporation doing the investing, and the nationality of the ultimate owner of the equity income. The existing international tax regime could be consistent with, although certainly does not achieve, this result because countries of residence adopt some form of relief from double taxation. As in the case of a set of export subsidies offsetting import tariffs, this system reduces trade distortions although it creates nettlesome issues of transfers between the importing and exporting countries.

The fact that a central feature of U.S. international tax policy—double tax relief is best viewed as part of a multilateral understanding that supports free trade makes it problematic to evaluate the ancillary characteristics of that policy. In cases where they conflict, what criterion should be used to evaluate tax policy? Should it be unilateral national income maximization, with the presumption that adherence to double taxation relief and nondiscrimination fulfills the country's obligations to free trade, or should the United States seek to extend the range of policies that, if adopted multilaterally, can—by enhancing free trade in capital— potentially lead to increased prosperity in the United States and abroad?

Income shifting and tax havens are critical problems for an international tax system that relies on source-based taxation. It is important for the U.S. tax system to defend its revenues with policy and enforcement measures that are more stringent than those applied to domestic compliance. The United States should also pursue multilateral means to harmonize corporate tax rates so as to reduce the incentives for income shifting and the reward to tax havens that practice "predatory tax protectionism." There is no reason, from either a global or a national perspective, that U.S.-parented multinational enterprises should pay more tax than a foreign-parented group with similar operations, but neither is there a compelling argument for tax breaks on the grounds of "ownership protectionism." Finally, although both a territorial and a worldwide system of taxation could be consistent with global free trade, there are important differences between the two systems. The territorial system is simpler and more likely to avoid a penalty for U.S. ownership but also more likely to encourage divergent worldwide tax rates and therefore deviations from free trade. Perhaps the most critical question is whether a territorial system can be as effective as a worldwide system in defending against predatory tax protectionism in the form of income shifting.

## REFERENCES

Ault, H. 1992. "Corporate integration and tax treaties: Where do we go from here?" *Tax Notes International*.

Ault, H., and D. Bradford. 1990. "Taxing international income: An analysis of the U.S. system and its economic premises." In *Taxation in the Global Economy*, A. Razin and J. Slemrod, eds. Chicago: University of Chicago Press and National Bureau of Economic Research.

Blumenthal, M., and J. Slemrod. 1995. "The compliance cost of taxing foreign-source income: Its magnitude, determinants and policy implications." Pp. 37-53 in *International Tax and Public Finance*; Also appears in *The Taxation of Multinational Corporations*, J. Slemrod, ed. Boston: Kluwer Academic Publishers, 1996.

Deardorff, A.V., and R.M. Stern. 1987. "Current issues in trade policy: An overview." In *U.S. Trade Policies in a Changing World Economy*, R.M. Stern, ed. Cambridge, Mass.: MIT Press.

Diamond, Peter, and James Mirrlees. 1971. "Optimal taxation and public production. I: Production efficiency." *American Economic Review* 8-27.

Dunning, J.H. 1985. *Multinational Enterprises, Economic Structure, and International Competitiveness,* J. H. Dunning, ed. Clichester: Wiley.

Frisch, D.J. 1990. "The economics of international tax policy: Some old and new approaches." *Tax Notes* (April):581-591.

Goodspeed, T.J., and D.J. Frisch. 1989. *"U.S. Tax Policy and the Overseas Activities of U.S. Multinational Corporations: A Quantitative Assessment."* Washington, D.C.: U.S Department of the Treasury, Office of Tax Analysis.

Gordon, R. 1986. "Taxation of investment and saving in a world economy." *American Economic Review* 1086-1102.

Grubert, H., and J. Mutti. 1987. "The impact of the tax reform act of 1986 on trade and capital flows." In *Compendium of Tax Research 1987.* Washington, D.C.: Office of Tax Analysis, U.S. Department of the Treasury.

Grubert, H., and J. Mutti. 1995. "Taxing Multinationals in a World with Portfolio Flows and R&D: Is Capital Export Neutrality Obsolete?" *International Tax and Public Finance* 293-317.

Grubert, H., and J. Mutti. 1996. "Do taxes influence where U.S. corporations invest?" paper presented at the Conference of the Trans-Atlantic Public Economics Seminar, Amsterdam, May 29-31, revised August.

Grubert, H., and J. Slemrod. Forthcoming. "Tax effects on investment and income shifting to Puerto Rico." *Review of Economics and Statistics.*

Grubert, H., W.C. Randolph, and D.J. Rousslang. 1996. "Country and multinational company responses to the tax reform act of 1986." *National Tax Journal* (September):341-358.

Harris, D., R. Morck, J. Slemrod, and B. Yeung. 1993. "Income shifting in U.S. multinational corporations." In *Studies in International Taxation,* A. Giovannini, R.G. Hubbard, and J. Slemrod, eds. Chicago: University of Chicago Press.

Hartman, D.E. 1985. "Tax policy and foreign direct investment." *Journal of Public Economics* 107-121.

Hines, J.R., Jr. 1996. "Altered states: Taxes and the location of foreign direct investment in America." *American Economic Review* 1076-1094.

Hines, J.R., Jr. 1997. "Tax policy and the activities of multinational corporations." In *Fiscal Policy: Lessons from Economic Research,* A. Auerbach, ed. Cambridge, Mass.: MIT Press.

Jun, J. 1989. *What Is the Marginal Source of Funds for Foreign Investment?* Working paper no. 3064. Cambridge, Mass.: National Bureau of Economic Research. August.

Krugman, P.R., and M. Obstfeld. 1991. *International Economics: Theory and Policy,* 2nd ed. New York: Harper Collins.

Leamer, E.E. 1996. "What do we know about the impact of offshore investment on the U.S. economy?" In *The Taxation of Multinational Corporations,* J. Slemrod, ed. New York: Kluwer Academic Press.

Levinsohn, J., and J. Slemrod. 1993. "Taxes, tariffs, and the global corporation." *Journal of Public Economics* (May):97-116.

Richman, P. 1963. *Taxation of Foreign Investment: An Economic Analysis.* Baltimore: Johns Hopkins Press.

Robinson, J. 1947. *Essays in the Theory of Employment.* Oxford: Blackwell.

Schmidt, W.E. 1975. "U.S. capital export policy: Backdoor mercantilism." *U.S. Taxation of American Business Abroad.* Washington, D.C.: American Enterprise Institute.

Slemrod, J. 1988. "Effect of taxation with international capital mobility." *Uneasy Compromise: Problems of a Hybrid Income Consumption Tax.* Washington, D.C.: Brookings Institution.

Slemrod, J. 1990a. "Tax principles in an international economy." In *World Tax Reform,* M. Boskin and C.E. McLure, Jr., eds. San Francisco: ICS Press.

Slemrod, J. 1990b. "The impact of the tax reform act of 1986 on foreign direct investment to and from the United States." In *Do Taxes Matter? The Impact of the Tax Reform Act of 1986,* J. Slemrod ed. Cambridge, Mass.: MIT Press.

Slemrod, J. 1994. "A General Model of the Behavioral Response to Taxation." Mimeograph. University of Michigan.

Slemrod, J. 1995. "Free trade taxation and protectionist taxation." *International Tax and Public Finance* 471-489.

Slemrod, J. 1997. "Comments on tax policy and the activities of multinational corporations by James R. Hines, Jr." In *Fiscal Policy: Lessons from Economic Research,* A. Auerbach, ed. Cambridge, Mass.: MIT Press

Tillinghast, D.R. 1991. "International tax simplification." *American Journal of Tax Policy* 8(2):187-247.

# 2

# International Taxation and Corporate R&D: Evidence and Implications[1]

JAMES R. HINES, JR.
*University of Michigan and
the National Bureau of Economic Research*

## INTRODUCTION

Governments design tax systems to pursue multiple objectives, including those of raising tax revenue, distributing tax burdens fairly, and providing appropriate economic incentives. Investment in research and development is generally thought to create unusually large positive economic spillovers; accordingly, it is afforded more favorable tax treatment than other investments such as those in plant and equipment. In the United States, most R&D expenses are deductible from current taxable income in calculating tax liabilities. In addition, enterprises may qualify to receive the research and experimentation tax credit. Furthermore, U.S.-based R&D directed at foreign markets for which American firms receive payment in the form of foreign-source royalties may receive favorable tax treatment in certain circumstances. Other advanced industrial countries offer similar types of tax-based encouragement of private-sector R&D (U.S. Congress, 1995; Organization for Economic Cooperation and Development, 1996).[2]

The eagerness of governments to use their tax systems to encourage domestic R&D, and thereby reap the economic benefits of R&D spillovers, is sometimes diminished by the multinational nature of modern businesses in high-technology industries. It is possible that the benefits of R&D undertaken in one country may generate economic spillovers in another. If so, governments may be somewhat less willing to grant as favorable tax treatment as if spillover benefits

[1]The author thanks James Poterba for helpful comments on an earlier draft.

[2]Virtually all countries permit firms to deduct R&D expenses immediately against their taxable incomes, and most provide supplemental credits, deductions, or other fiscal inducements to undertake R&D. Germany and the United Kingdom are notable exceptions in providing no fiscal incentives other than immediate deductibility of R&D expenses.

*39*

were concentrated in the location in which R&D is undertaken. Since very little is known about the nature of technology spillovers, it is also possible that the local benefits generated by R&D performed by domestically owned firms are not the same as those generated by R&D performed by foreign-owned firms. Since the reality of modern industrial life is that most private-sector R&D is undertaken by multinational firms, whether owned locally or by foreigners, government policies must be crafted in environments in which there are spillovers between domestic and foreign markets but uncertainty concerning their magnitudes. The purpose of this chapter is to review the history of U.S. tax policy toward research activities undertaken by multinational firms in the United States and the available evidence on its impact.

## THE TAX TREATMENT OF MULTINATIONAL CORPORATIONS[3]

The United States taxes income on a residence basis, meaning that American corporations and individuals owe taxes to the U.S. government on all of their worldwide incomes. The top U.S. corporate tax rate is now 35 percent. Since profits earned in foreign countries are usually taxed by host governments, U.S. law permits taxpayers to claim tax credits for foreign income taxes and related tax obligations in order to avoid subjecting American multinationals to double taxation. The foreign tax credit mechanism implies that a U.S. corporation earning $100 in a foreign country with a 12 percent tax rate (and a foreign tax obligation of $12) pays only $23 to the U.S. government, since its U.S. corporate tax liability of $35 (35 percent of $100) is reduced to $23 by the foreign tax credit of $12. The foreign tax credit is, however, limited to U.S. tax liability on foreign income. If, in the example, the foreign tax rate were 50 percent, the firm would pay $50 to the foreign government, but its U.S. foreign tax credit would be limited to $35. Hence, an American firm receives full tax credits for its foreign taxes paid only when it is in a deficit credit position (i.e., when its average foreign tax rate is less than its tax rate on domestic operations). A firm has excess credits if its available foreign tax credits exceed U.S. tax liability on its foreign income. Firms combine their taxable incomes and taxes paid in all of their foreign operations in calculating their foreign tax credits and the foreign tax credit limit.[4]

---

[3]Portions of this description of U.S. tax law are excerpted from Hines (1991).

[4]In order to qualify for the foreign tax credit, firms must own at least 10 percent of a foreign affiliate, and only those taxes that qualify as income taxes are creditable. Furthermore, income is broken into different functional "baskets" in the calculation of applicable credits and limits. Income earned and taxes paid in the conduct of most types of active foreign business operations are grouped in one basket; petroleum industry income is grouped in a separate basket; and there are separate baskets for items such as passive income earned abroad. The basket distinctions imply that a firm might simultaneously have excess foreign tax credits in the petroleum basket (which is common, since foreign tax rates on oil income are typically quite high) and deficit foreign tax credits in the active income basket. Such a firm would have to pay some U.S. tax on its active foreign income, even though it has excess foreign tax credits on its petroleum income.

Deferral of U.S. taxation of certain foreign earnings is another important feature of the U.S. international tax system. Generally, an American parent firm is taxed on its subsidiaries' foreign income only when this is repatriated to the parent corporation. This type of deferral is available only to foreign operations that are separately incorporated in foreign countries (subsidiaries of the parent), not to consolidated (branch) operations. The U.S. government taxes branch profits as they are earned, just as it does profits earned within the United States.

The deferral of U.S. taxation may create incentives for firms with lightly taxed foreign earnings to delay repatriating dividends from their foreign subsidiaries.[5] In some cases, firms expect never to repatriate their foreign earnings. In other cases, they may anticipate that future years will be more attractive for repatriation either because domestic tax rates will be lower or because future sources of foreign income will generate excess foreign tax credits that can be used to offset U.S. tax liability on the dividends.[6] It appears that in practice, U.S. multinationals choose their dividend repatriations selectively, generally paying dividends out of their more heavily taxed foreign earnings first.[7] Consequently, the average tax rate that firms face on their foreign income need not exactly equal the average foreign tax rate faced by their branches and subsidiaries abroad.

Branch earnings and dividends from subsidiaries represent only two forms of foreign income for U.S. income tax purposes. Interest received from foreign sources also represents foreign income, although foreign interest receipts are often classified in their own basket and hence are not combined with other income in calculating the foreign tax credit. Royalty income received from foreigners, including foreign affiliates of U.S. firms, is also foreign-source income. Foreign governments often impose moderate taxes on dividend, interest, and royalty payments from foreign affiliates to their American parent companies; these withholding[8] taxes are fully creditable against an American taxpayer's U.S. tax liability on foreign income.

---

[5]The incentive to defer repatriation of lightly taxed subsidiary earnings is attenuated by the subpart F provisions introduced in U.S. law in 1962, that treat a subsidiary's passive income and income invested in U.S. property as if they were distributed to its American owners, thereby subjecting such income to immediate U.S. taxation. Subpart F rules apply to controlled foreign corporations, which are foreign corporations owned at least 50 percent by U.S. persons holding stakes of at least 10 percent each. Controlled foreign corporations that earn and reinvest their foreign earnings in active businesses can continue to defer their U.S. tax liability on those earnings. See Hines and Rice (1994) and Scholes and Wolfson (1992) for the behavioral implications of these rules.

[6]It is interesting to note that the deferral of U.S. tax liability does not itself create an incentive to delay paying dividends from foreign subsidiaries since the U.S. tax must be paid eventually (see Hartman, 1985).

[7]See the evidence presented in Hines and Hubbard (1990), Altshuler and Newlon (1993), and Altshuler et al. (1995).

[8]Taxes on cross-border flows, such as dividends, interest, and royalties, are known as "withholding" taxes due to some of the niceties of their administration. Strictly speaking, these taxes represent obligations of the recipients and not the payors; this arrangement permits immediate crediting of withholding taxes by recipients who are eligible to claim foreign tax credits. The taxes are called withholding taxes because the local payor is the withholding agent for the tax and is therefore liable to ensure that the taxes are paid.

Royalties received by American parent firms for R&D used abroad represent taxable foreign-source income of the American firms. American firms with deficit foreign tax credits must pay U.S. income tax on these royalty receipts, whereas firms with excess foreign tax credits may be able to apply the excess credits against U.S. taxes due on the royalties, thereby eliminating the U.S. tax liability otherwise created by the royalty receipts.

Most of the world's governments impose withholding taxes on cross-border royalty payments from affiliates located within their countries. These royalty tax rates are frequently reduced under the terms of bilateral tax treaties. For example, the United States imposes a 30 percent tax on royalties paid to foreign corporations, but this tax rate is often reduced, in some cases to zero, when recipients of royalty payments are located in countries with whom the United States has a tax treaty in force.

### Interaction of R&D and Foreign Income Rules

American firms with foreign income are generally not permitted to deduct all of their R&D expenditures in the United States against their domestic taxable incomes. Instead, the law provides for various methods of allocating R&D expenses between domestic and foreign income.

The intention of the law is to retain the relatively generous treatment of R&D only for that part of a firm's R&D expenditures that is devoted to production for domestic markets. R&D-performing firms with foreign sales and foreign income are presumed to be doing at least some of their R&D to enhance their foreign profitability.

From the standpoint of taxpaying firms, U.S. tax law's distinction between domestic and foreign R&D deductions is potentially quite important. If an R&D expense is deemed to be domestic, it is deductible against the taxpayer's U.S. taxable income. Alternatively, if it is deemed to be foreign, the R&D expense reduces foreign taxable income *for the purposes of U.S. income taxation only.* Foreign governments do not use U.S. methods of calculating R&D deductions and generally do not permit American firms to reduce their taxable incomes in foreign countries on the basis of R&D undertaken in the United States. Consequently, an R&D expense deduction allocated against foreign income is valuable to an American firm only if the firm has deficit foreign tax credits. If the firm has deficit credits, then the firm pays some U.S. tax on its foreign income, and any additional dollar of R&D deduction allocated against foreign income reduces the firm's U.S. taxable income by a dollar.[9] Firms with deficit foreign tax credits are therefore indifferent between allocating R&D expenses against foreign income

---

[9]Curiously, the law is written so that the additional dollar of R&D deduction reduces taxable income without reducing the foreign tax credits available for foreign income taxes paid.

and allocating them against domestic income.[10] By contrast, firms with excess foreign tax credits pay no U.S. tax on their foreign income and therefore have no use for R&D deductions allocated against foreign income. Consequently, firms with excess foreign tax credits lose the value of any R&D deductions allocated against foreign income.

It is important to consider the tax treatment of royalties together with any evaluation of the impact of the R&D expense allocation rules. American firms with excess foreign tax credits that undertake R&D in the United States directed at enhancing profitability in foreign markets are unable to recieve full deductions for their U.S. R&D expenses, but they are able to receive their returns in the form of foreign-source royalty receipts that are untaxed by the United States due to their excess foreign tax credits. Consequently, U.S. tax law discourages such firms from undertaking R&D directed at domestic markets while encouraging such firms to undertake R&D directed at foreign markets. Of course, in practice, R&D-performing firms may not always be in positions to know whether particular R&D projects are more likely to generate domestic or foreign income when and if ultimately successful.

## HISTORY OF U.S. R&D ALLOCATION RULES[11]

The tax law governing the allocation of R&D expenses was for years rather vague but was codified by U.S. Treasury Regulation section 1.861-8 in 1977. The 1977 rules provide for several stages in allocating R&D expenses for tax purposes. Research and development in the United States that is undertaken to meet certain legal requirements such as complying with pollution standards can be allocated 100 percent against domestic income. Firms that perform more than half of their other than legally required R&D in the United States are permitted to allocate 30 percent of that R&D against U.S. income. The remaining 70 percent is then to be allocated between domestic and foreign sources on the basis of sales, including the sales of controlled foreign corporations. Research and development is generally allocated to activities within product lines (defined in a manner comparable to two-digit SIC codes), so that a corporation need not allocate part of its chemical R&D against foreign income simply because the electronics part of its business has foreign sales.

There are several options available to taxpayers who are unsatisfied with the outcome of the R&D allocation method just described. Firms are permitted to apportion more than 30 percent of their domestic R&D against U.S. income if

---

[10]This statement, along with much of the analysis described in this chapter, abstracts from the ability of firms to carry excess foreign tax credits backward two years and forward five years. Firms that can exploit carryforwards or carrybacks may (depending on specific circumstances) face incentives that are intermediate between those of deficit credit and excess credit firms.

[11]Portions of this brief description of U.S. law are excerpted from Hines (1994).

they can establish that it is reasonable to expect the R&D so apportioned to have very limited application outside the country; the remaining portion of their R&D expenses are then allocated on the basis of sales. Alternatively, firms are permitted to allocate their R&D on the basis of total foreign and domestic income, although without the 30 percent initial allocation to U.S. source, so that firms with foreign operations that generate sales but not income relative to domestic operations might prefer the income allocation method. There is, however, a limit to the income allocation method: firms are not permitted to reduce their foreign-source R&D expense allocation to less than 50 percent of the allocation that would have been produced by the sales method, including the 30 percent initial apportionment.

The Economic Recovery Tax Act in 1981 changed these rules by permitting American firms to allocate 100 percent of the expense of R&D performed in the United States against U.S. taxable income. This change was intended to offer strong R&D incentives while affording Congress the opportunity to rethink its R&D policy for two years. At the end of that time, the U.S. Department of the Treasury (1983) produced a study concluding that the tax change presented a small R&D incentive to U.S. firms and was desirable on that basis.[12] In 1984 and 1985, Congress extended the temporary change permitting 100 percent allocation of U.S. R&D expenses to U.S. income, so these rules remained in place until the end of the 1986 tax year.

The Tax Reform Act of 1986 removed the 100 percent allocation of U.S. R&D expenses, replacing it with a new, and again temporary, system of R&D expense allocation.[13] Under the 1986 act, 50 percent of U.S. R&D expense (other than for R&D to meet regulatory requirements) was allocated to domestic-source income, with the remaining 50 percent allocated on the basis of sales or income, at the taxpayer's choice. There was no limit imposed on the degree to which allocation on the basis of gross income could reduce foreign allocation relative to the sales method.

The Technical and Miscellaneous Revenue Act of 1988 changed the R&D expense allocation rules for the first part of 1988. For the first four months of the year, firms were permitted to allocate 64 percent of U.S. R&D expense against U.S. domestic income, with the remaining 36 percent allocated between foreign and domestic sources on the basis of either sales or income, at the taxpayer's choice. The 1988 act further provided that if the 36 percent was allocated on the

---

[12]The Treasury Department (1983) study based its conclusions on a range of assumed elasticities of R&D with respect to price changes; no attempt was made to ascertain how firms responded to the changes introduced in 1981.

[13]The Tax Reform Act of 1986 also introduced a number of other changes relevant to R&D investment decisions, including reducing the statutory corporate tax rate from 46 percent (the tax rate from 1979 to 1986) to 40 percent in 1987 and 34 percent for 1988 and subsequent years. The 1986 act also removed a number of investment incentives such as accelerated depreciation of capital assets and the investment tax credit for new equipment purchases.

basis of income, the R&D allocation against foreign income must equal at least 30 percent of the foreign allocation that would have been produced by the sales method. For the remaining eight months of the year, taxpayers were required to use the allocation method described in section 1.861-8 as of 1977 and also described above.

The Omnibus Budget Reconciliation Act of 1989 again changed the R&D allocation rules, this time reintroducing the same rules that applied for the first four months of 1988. The Omnibus Budget Reconciliation Act of 1990 and the Tax Extension Act of 1991 extended this treatment of R&D expenses until a date that depends on a taxpayer's choice of fiscal year, but in no case later than August 1, 1992. Consequently, 64 percent of domestically performed R&D in 1989-1992 could be allocated against domestic income, with the remaining 36 percent allocated on the basis either of sales or of income, although use of the income method could not reduce foreign-source allocation to less than 30 percent of the foreign-source allocation that would have been produced by the sales method.

Expiration of the R&D expense allocation legislation in the summer of 1992 motivated an extensive reconsideration of the issue of the appropriate tax treatment of R&D expenditures by multinational firms. In June 1992, the Treasury Department temporarily suspended its section 1.861-8 allocation rules (the 1977 regulations), replacing them with an 18-month moratorium in which taxpayers could continue to use the system in effect from 1989 to 1992: 64 percent place-of-performance allocation, with the remaining deductions allocated on the basis of sales or income. The department was to reexamine its section 1.861-8 regulations during the 18-month period. The explanation for the moratorium was "to provide taxpayers with transition relief and to minimize audit controversy and facilitate business planning during the conduct of the regulatory review" (U.S. Congress, 1993). Some contemporaneous observers noted that extension of the R&D allocation rules through Treasury Department moratorium instead of legislation made the rules less costly from the standpoint of federal budget targets since regulatory changes are exempt from the budget agreement limits. What role, if any, such considerations played in the decision to suspend the section 1.861-8 rules is not clear. In any case, the moratorium did not run its full course, being supplanted in 1993 by new legislation.

President Clinton's budget proposal of February 1993 recommended a major change in the allocation of R&D expenditures and the treatment of royalty receipts by U.S.-based multinational corporations. The President proposed that American firms deduct 100 percent of their U.S. R&D expenditures against U.S. income but that the same firms no longer be permitted to use foreign tax credits generated by their active foreign operations to reduce U.S. tax liabilities on royalty income from foreign sources. Instead, firms would be required to allocate foreign-source royalty income to the passive basket in determining their foreign tax credit limits. The administration's intention was to limit severely the ability of American firms to use excess foreign tax credits to reduce their U.S. tax liabilities on foreign-source royalty income. Very few firms have excess foreign tax credits in the passive basket.

Instead, the Omnibus Budget Reconciliation Act of 1993 (OBRA 93) continued the pattern of allowing U.S.-based multinational firms to allocate only a fraction of their U.S. R&D expenses to U.S. income and, at the same time, permitted firms to use foreign tax credits to eliminate U.S. tax liabilities on foreign-source royalty income. OBRA 93 permitted firms to allocate 50 percent of U.S.-based R&D expenses to domestic source, with the remaining 50 percent allocated between domestic and foreign source based either on sales or on income, at the taxpayer's option-subject to the restriction that income-based allocation not reduce foreign-source allocation to less than 30 percent of that produced by the sales method. The allocation rules under OBRA 93 were temporary, expiring one year after they took effect. Many observers attributed the temporary nature of the allocation rules to the mechanics of compliance with federal budget targets. If Congress were to pass permanent legislation covering the R&D allocation rules, the "cost" to the current-year budget of any treatment more generous than the 1977 regulations must include costs incurred in future years. By instead passing temporary legislation, Congress incurs budgetary costs only for the current year. Of course, budgetary costs need not bear any relation to the economic consequences of permanent legislation covering the allocation of R&D expenses.[14]

During 1995, the Treasury Department reconsidered the appropriateness of its 1977 R&D expense regulations. Based on newer analysis (U.S. Department of the Treasury, 1995), the regulations were amended roughly along the lines of recent legislative developments. Specifically, the 1995 regulations permit firms to select one of two allocation methods, the first allowing firms to allocate 50 percent of U.S.-based R&D expenses to domestic source with the remaining 50 percent allocated between domestic and foreign sources based on sales, and the second method permitting firms to allocate 25 percent of U.S.-based R&D expenses to domestic source with the remaining 75 percent allocated between domestic and foreign source based on gross income. Under these regulations, income-based allocation is not permitted to reduce foreign-source allocation to less than 50 percent of that produced by the sales method.[15] Since the OBRA 93

---

[14]Some people strongly believe that permanent legislation creates a more predictable environment for businesses, thereby making the United States a more attractive location for R&D. Turro (1993, p. 436) quotes one tax practitioner, who describes the Congress's decision to make the OBRA 93 R&D allocation rules temporary an "absurd tax policy decision."

[15]The new regulations amend the previous rules in certain, more minor, ways. Specifically, firms generally are required to make their elections permanent, so it is not possible to use the sales method in one year and the income method in the next. In addition, the new regulations specify that firms allocate R&D expenses based on three-digit SIC activities, rather than the two-digit SIC activities provided in the previous regulations.

R&D allocation rules have expired, the 1995 Treasury Department regulations now govern the allocation of U.S. R&D expenses.[16]

## Quantitative Impact of Tax Rules

The tax treatment of R&D and royalty income clearly influences the incentives American and foreign firms face in undertaking R&D in the United States and abroad. There remains the question of the extent to which levels of R&D activity respond to these incentives. This is a difficult question to evaluate fully, since R&D activity depends not only on the tax treatment of R&D per se but also on the tax treatment of other domestic and foreign investments, government-sponsored R&D efforts, the technological sophistication of local economies, the cost of technology inputs, and a host of other variables. In spite of these contributing factors, it is nevertheless possible to find quantitative evidence of the responsiveness of R&D to its tax treatment.

For years the received wisdom of the academic literature was that the own-price demand elasticity of R&D was relatively small in absolute value, on the order of 0.5 or smaller.[17] More recent estimates of Hines (1993) and Hall (1993) find elasticities of unity or greater in absolute value.[18] The significance of an elasticity larger than unity in absolute value is that it implies that a tax benefit for R&D stimulates more additional private-sector R&D than the amount of forgone tax revenue.

Hines (1993) uses firm-specific changes after 1986 in the tax cost of undertaking R&D in the United States, based on changes in the R&D expense allocation rules, to estimate the responsiveness of R&D spending to its after-tax cost. The study analyzes two samples of large firms between 1984 and 1989—the first, a sample of 40 firms that experienced no merger activity, and the second, a sample of 116 firms that includes those with minor merger activity. In both samples, the R&D expenditures of firms with significant foreign sales and excess foreign tax credits grow systematically more slowly after 1986 than do the R&D expenditures of other firms. The implied price elasticity of R&D is –1.8 in the 40-firm subsample and –0.8 in the 116-firm sample. Given the omission of variables to

---

[16]It is noteworthy that the 1995 revisions to the R&D cost allocation regulations were not "costly" from the standpoint of federal budget targets since regulatory changes are not budgeted.

[17]See, for example, Bernstein and Nadiri (1989), who estimate R&D price elasticities to be between –0.4 and –0.5 for a sample of manufacturing firms, whereas Nadiri and Prucha (1989) find the R&D price elasticity to be much closer to zero for the U.S. Bell System. In a study of Canadian firms, Bernstein (1985) reports estimated R&D price elasticities of between –0.1 and –0.4. Mansfield (1986) and the U.S. General Accounting Office (1989) summarize the literature with the conclusion that the consensus range of price elasticities is –0.2 to –0.5.

[18]A literature survey by the U.S. General Accounting Office (1996) concludes that on the basis of these and other recent studies, the consensus range of price elasticities of demand for R&D in the United States was higher by 1996 than it was in 1989.

control for merger effects in the larger sample, the true elasticity is probably closer to –1.8 than to –0.8.  An own-price elasticity of R&D in that range is much larger than those reported by earlier studies but is consistent with Hall's (1993) firm-level study of domestic responses to incentives created by the research and experimentation tax credit.

The available evidence indicates that there is little change over time in the fraction of total R&D that American firms perform abroad, which is roughly constant at about 10 percent.[19]  One might wonder why this ratio would remain constant over a period that includes the 1986 U.S. tax changes that reduce the deductibility of domestic R&D expenses if indeed there is an elasticity of demand for R&D in the neighborhood of unity.   Hines (1994) argues that such a large elasticity is consistent with an unchanged ratio of foreign to domestic R&D by American firms because the same 1986 tax change that reduced the deductibility of domestic R&D expenses also made foreign-source royalty income more attractive by increasing the number of American firms with excess foreign tax credits. The tax change discouraged American firms from undertaking R&D in the United States directed at domestic markets and encouraged R&D directed at foreign markets.  There was little net effect of these two changes on the total volume of R&D in the United States, although of course firms with different tax situations and those operating in distinct markets were affected differently.

It is possible to use estimated response elasticities to project the effects of various possible tax reforms on tax revenue and R&D activity.  Although such exercises are of necessity partial equilibrium in nature and rely on imprecisely estimated parameters, they offer the benefit of illustrating the trade-offs implicit in the current tax treatment of R&D.  Table 2.1, which is drawn from Hines (1993), indicates changes in U.S. corporate tax revenue and U.S.-based R&D activity that would accompany two alternative reforms, if prevailing corporate activity and U.S. tax law as of 1989 are assumed.  The first reform is one in which American multinational firms would be permitted to deduct 100 percent of their domestic R&D expenses against their taxable U.S. incomes; the second is one in which the R&D expenses of American multinationals would be allocated between domestic and foreign sources on the basis of relative sales without any adjustment for place of R&D performance.  Complete domestic deductibility of R&D expense reduces corporate tax collections by $1.2 billion while encouraging an additional $2.2 billion of private-sector R&D by affected firms. The alternative of R&D expense allocation on the basis of sales generates an additional $2.5 billion of tax revenue while reducing private-sector R&D by $2.6 billion.

These results suggest that the current tax treatment of R&D expenses of U.S.-based multinational firms displaces private-sector R&D by an amount that is roughly the same order of magnitude as the tax revenue it generates.  Although

---

[19]See the evidence presented in Hines (1994).

**TABLE 2.1**  Estimated Effects of Two Policy Reforms on R&D and Tax Revenue[a]

| Contemplated Reform | Change in Tax Revenue (million dollars) | Change in R&D (million dollars) |
|---|---|---|
| 100 percent domestic deductibility of R&D expenses | −1,166 | 2,230 |
| Pure sales apportionment of R&D expenses | 2,542 | −2,590 |

Figures are based on an analysis of 189 multinational firms with $41 billion of R&D expenditures in 1989, as reported in Hines (1993). Firms are assumed currently to use the sales apportionment method to allocate their R&D expense deductions.

[a]Note: Entries are millions of current dollars in 1989.

the details of alternative tax reform proposals differ in many particulars including their treatment of average and marginal R&D expenses, the trade-off of private-sector R&D for tax revenue is unlikely to differ greatly from the range of, say, 1-2.5 due to the approximately unit elastic responsiveness of R&D to its after-tax price. Although this calculation omits various important considerations such as the long-run effect of the tax treatment of R&D on the entry and exit of firms into technology-intensive industries, the taxation of alternative uses of resources that would otherwise be devoted to R&D, and others, it captures one of the important considerations in the design of R&D tax policy: the trade-off between private incentives and public tax revenues.

## INTERNATIONAL TECHNOLOGY FLOWS AND GOVERNMENT POLICY

Government policy has the ability to influence the incentives firms have to undertake R&D and to use the technology produced by research in domestic and foreign markets. One of the lively policy questions is the degree to which technology developed in one country influences economic activity in another. A related question is one of the degree to which R&D activities undertaken in different countries substitute for each other.

The limited available evidence suggests that there is extensive international use of locally developed technology. American firms perform only about 10 percent of their R&D abroad, but foreign-source royalties received by Americans for technology and know-how exported abroad greatly exceed their foreign R&D. In 1991, American firms received $17.8 billion in foreign-source royalties while spending $8.7 billion on R&D abroad. Over recent years the difference between these two figures has grown every year.[20]

---

[20]See the evidence reported in Hines (1994).

Foreign investors in the United States transfer technology to their U.S. operations in two forms, through technology for which royalties are paid and also through R&D performed locally in the United States. The magnitude of the latter is quite large, reflecting the technological nature of the industries in which foreign investors concentrate. In every year since 1982, foreign investors have performed more R&D in the United States than American firms have undertaken abroad.[21]

The linkage between technology transfer and accompanying royalties provides an opportunity to draw useful inferences about the degree of substitutability between domestic and foreign R&D. Domestic R&D generates technologies that foreign affiliates can use in return for paying royalties. Policies that make royalty payments more expensive thereby reduce the usefulness of domestic R&D for foreign operations. Hence, to the extent that foreign operations respond to higher costs of royalty payments by increasing their own R&D intensities, it follows that domestic and foreign R&D are substitutes. In such circumstances, domestic policies that increase the cost of R&D have the effect of driving R&D activity offshore.

Hines (1995) investigates these issues by estimating the effect of royalty withholding taxes on R&D performed by foreign subsidiaries. Since foreign subsidiaries are required to pay royalties to their parent companies for imported technology, higher royalty taxes, even if partly avoided by adept transfer pricing, raise the cost of technology imports. Higher costs of imported technology stimulate local R&D if the two are substitutes and discourage R&D if they are complements. Cross-sectional estimates of R&D intensities of the foreign operations of U.S. firms in 43 countries in 1989 indicate a cross-elasticity of 0.16, suggesting that R&D and imported technology are substitutes. Cross-sectional estimates of the R&D activities of foreign-owned firms in the United States in 1987 indicate a somewhat larger cross-elasticity, 0.30, which likewise suggests that imported technology and locally produced technology are substitutes. The implication of these results is that R&D cost allocation rules, the tax treatment of royalties, and other tax policies that influence levels of domestic R&D also influence the foreign R&D activities of American firms.

It is a mistake to evaluate tax policies or any other government policies in isolation since so many things that governments do influence economic behavior in general and R&D activity in particular. The purpose of this chapter is to review some of the U.S. international tax policies that most directly affect domestic and foreign R&D. The R&D expense allocation rules and the tax treatment of royalties recieved from abroad are two of the most important of these policies. The quantitative evidence indicates that tax policies influence significantly the level, composition, and location of R&D activity. Those who design future U.S. tax policy toward R&D are well advised to bear in mind the responsiveness of this activity in selecting the direction of U.S. policy.

---

[21]See the evidence reported in Hines (1995).

## REFERENCES

Altshuler, R., and T.S. Newlon. 1993. "The effects of U.S. tax policy on the income repatriation patterns of U.S. multinational corporations." Pp.77-115 in *Studies in International Taxation,* A. Giovannini, R.G. Hubbard, and J. Slemrod, eds. Chicago, Ill.: University of Chicago Press.

Altshuler, R., T.S. Newlon, and W.C. Randolph. 1995. "Do repatriation taxes matter? Evidence from the tax returns of U.S. multinationals." Pp. 253-272 in *The Effects of Taxation on Multinational Corporations,* M. Feldstein, J.R. Hines Jr., and R.G. Hubbard, eds. Chicago, Ill.: University of Chicago Press.

Bernstein, J. I. 1985. "Research and development, patents, and grant and tax policies in Canada." Pp. 1-41 in *Technological Change in Canadian Industry,* D.G. McFetridge, ed. Toronto: University of Toronto Press.

Bernstein, J. I. and M.I. Nadiri. 1989. "Rates of return on physical and R&D capital and structure of production process: Cross section and time series evidence." Pp. 169-187 in *Advances in Econometrics and Modeling,* Baldev Raj, ed. Dordrecht, the Netherlands: Kluwer.

Hall, B.H. 1993. "R&D tax policy during the 1980s: Success or failure?" Pp. 1-35 in *Tax Policy and the Economy,* J. M. Poterba, ed. Vol. 7. Cambridge, Mass.: MIT Press.

Hartman, D.G. 1985. "Tax policy and foreign direct investment." *Journal of Public Economics* 26:107-121.

Hines, J.R., Jr. 1991. "The flight paths of migratory corporations." *Journal of Accounting, Auditing, and Finance* 6:447-479.

Hines, J.R., Jr 1993. "On the sensitivity of R&D to delicate tax changes: The behavior of U.S. multinationals in the 1980's." Pp. 149-187 in *Studies in International Taxation,* A. Giovannini, R.G. Hubbard, and J. Slemrod, eds. Chicago, Ill.: University of Chicago Press.

Hines, J.R., Jr. 1994. "No place like home: Tax incentives and the location of R&D by American multinationals." Pp. 65-104 in *Tax Policy and the Economy,* J. M. Poterba, ed. Vol. 8. Cambridge, Mass.: MIT Press.

Hines, J.R., Jr. 1995. "Taxes, technology transfer, and the R&D activities of multinational firms." Pp. 225-248 in *The Effects of Taxation on Multinational Corporations,* M. Feldstein, J.R. Hines, Jr., and R.G. Hubbard, eds. Chicago, Ill.: University of Chicago Press.

Hines, J.R., Jr., and R.G. Hubbard. 1990. "Coming home to America: Dividend repatriations by U.S. multiationals." Pp. 161-200 in *Taxation in the Global Economy,* A. Razin and J. Slemrod, eds. Chicago, Ill.: University of Chicago Press.

Hines, J.R., Jr. and E.M. Rice. 1994. "Fiscal paradise: foreign tax havens and American business." *Quarterly Journal of Economics* 109:149-182.

Mansfield, E. 1986. "The R&D tax credit and other technology policy issues." *American Economic Review* 76:190-194.

Mansfield, E., D. Teece, and A. Romeo. 1979 "Overseas research and development by U.S.-based firms." *Economica* 46:187-196.

Nadiri, M.I. and I.R. Prucha. 1989. "Dynamic factor demand models, productivity measurement, and rates of return: Theory and an empirical application to the U.S. Bell System." Working paper no. 3041. Cambridge, Mass.: National Bureau of Economic Research.

Organization for Economic Cooperation and Development. 1996. *Fiscal Measures to Promote R&D and Innovation.* ODCE/GD(96)165. Paris: OECD.

Scholes, M.S. and M.A. Wolfson. 1992. *Taxes and Business Strategy: A Planning Approach.* Englewood Cliffs, N.J.: Prentice Hall.

Turro, J. 1993. "U.S. enacts controversial budget legislation." *Tax Notes International* 16(7):435-438.

U.S. Congress, Joint Committee on Taxation. 1993. *Summary of the President's Revenue Proposals.* Washington, D.C.: U.S. Government Printing Office.

U.S. Congress, Office of Technology Assessment. 1995. *The Effectiveness of Research and Experimentation Tax Credits.* Washington, D.C.: U.S. Government Printing Office.

U.S. Department of the Treasury. 1983. *The Impact of the Section 861-8 Regulation on U.S. Research and Development.* Washington, D.C.: U.S. Government Printing Office.

U.S. Department of the Treasury. 1995. *The Relationship Between U.S. Research and Development and Foreign Income.* Washington, D.C.: U.S. Department of the Treasury.

U.S. General Accounting Office. 1989. *The Research Credit Has Stimulated Some Additional Research Spending.* Report GAO/GGD-89-114. Washington, D.C.: U.S. Government Printing Office.

U.S. General Accounting Office. 1996. R*eview of Studies of the Effectiveness of the Research Tax Credit.* Report GAO/GGD-96-43. Washington, D.C.: U.S. Government Printing Office.

# 3

# R&D Tax Incentives and Manufacturing-Sector R&D Expenditures

M. ISHAQ NADIRI
*New York University*

THEOFANIS P. MAMUNEAS
*University of Cyprus*

## INTRODUCTION

An important characteristic of R&D investment distinguishing it from other types of investment is that its output has the properties of public goods; it can be considered at least partially nonexcludable and nonrivalrous.[1] Indeed, the empirical literature provides extensive evidence that not only is the rate of return of privately funded R&D investment very high compared to that of investment in physical capital, but more importantly, its social rate of return is several times higher than its private rate of return.[2] This suggests that there are substantial externalities or spillover effects associated with R&D investment. Therefore, privately financed R&D is suboptimal, and the direct or indirect support of government is justified.

Theoretically, there are many different ways to deal with market failure associated with externalities. For instance, externality-generating activities can be encouraged by providing subsidies, by granting producers property rights and charging differential prices for their use by others, by allowing firms to internalize the externality, and finally, by having the government engage directly in externality-generating activity. Indeed, in the postwar period, the U.S. government has pursued a combination of these policies—strengthening innovators' property rights through the patent system; encouraging firms to form joint R&D ventures; directly investing in R&D through companies, universities, and other nonprofit in-

---

[1]See Arrow (1962), Spence (1984), and Romer (1990).

[2]See, for instance, Griliches (1979, 1991), Cohen and Levin (1989), Mohnen (1990), and Nadiri (1993).

stitutions and government laboratories; and lastly, providing tax incentives for company-financed R&D.

This chapter attempts to evaluate the contributions of R&D tax policies—in particular, the expensing of R&D and the research and experimentation (R&E) credit first instituted in 1981—in promoting R&D investment in U. S. manufacturing industries. Three specific public policy issues are addressed:

1. How much lower would private R&D investment have been if the R&E credit were abolished and if R&D expenditures were treated as amortizable capital expenditures similar to expenditures on plant and equipment?
2. What are the social benefit-cost ratios of these R&D tax policies over the period of the study?
3. Finally, what appear to be the potential shortcomings of the R&E tax credit and how might it be made more effective?

To answer these questions, we estimated a cost function, taking into account the level of output, prices of the traditional inputs such as labor and private capital, the rental price of company-financed R&D capital, and the capital stocks of publicly financed R&D.[3] Cost and factor demand functions for the private factors of production including industry-financed R&D capital stock are estimated jointly.[4] In this framework, input demands are interrelated; changes in the price of one input affect demand for other inputs. For example, changes in tax incentives for physical plant and equipment affect not only the demand for physical capital but also the decision to invest in R&D activities. Similarly, changes in the price of industry R&D capital may affect the demand for labor and physical capital. These cross-price elasticities are important in addition to each factor's price elasticities in evaluating the effects of public R&D policies.

The model is estimated using a sample of 15 manufacturing industries, which constitute the manufacturing sector, as reported in Table 3.1. These industries perform the bulk of R&D in the U.S. economy. Data on the quantities and price indices of output, labor, physical capital, and intermediate inputs were obtained from the Bureau of Labor Statistics, and R&D data were obtained from the National Science Foundation.[5] The estimation period covers the years 1956 to 1988. Using the estimates of the model, it is possible to calculate the output and price elasticities of the demand for various inputs and to measure the effects of government R&D tax and incentive policies on the costs and production structure of U.S. manufacturing industries.

---

[3]For specification and estimation of the model, see Mamuneas and Nadiri (1996).

[4]Two publicly financed R&D capital stocks also enter the cost function as shift variables and thereby affect demand for labor, capital and private R&D. One type of publicly financed R&D is performed inside a given industry, the second type is all other publicly financed R&D performed outside the particular industry. The latter captures potential spillover benefits from government-financed R&D activities. These publicly financed R&D stocks and the disembodied technical change have nonneutral effects on the structure of the industry cost and demand for inputs. (See Mamuneas and Nadiri, 1996)

[5]A description of the data is available upon request.

**TABLE 3.1**    Industry Classification

| Code | SIC Codes | Industry |
|------|-----------|----------|
| 20 | 20 | Food and kindred products |
| 26 | 26 | Paper and allied products |
| 28 | 28 | Chemicals and allied products |
| 29 | 29 | Petroleum refining and related industries |
| 30 | 30 | Rubber products |
| 32 | 32 | Stone, clay, and glass products |
| 33 | 33 | Primary metals |
| 34 | 34 | Fabricated metal products |
| 35 | 35 | Machinery |
| 36 | 36 | Electrical equipment |
| 37 | 37 | Transportation equipment |
| 38 | 38 | Scientific instruments |
| 40 | 22, 23 | Textiles and apparel |
| 41 | 24, 25 | Lumber, wood products, and furniture |
| 42 | 21, 27, 31, 39 | Other manufacturing industries |

## EFFECTS OF R&D TAX POLICY ON COST STRUCTURE

Historically, the federal government, recognizing the importance of R&D investment for economic growth and international competitiveness, has treated R&D investment more favorably than other kinds of investments. The federal government basically uses two types of tax policy instruments to stimulate R&D expenditures. One, in place since 1954, is the immediate deductibility provision of company-financed R&D expenditures. The second is the direct R&E tax credit introduced by the Economic Recovery Tax Act of 1981.

The 1981 Tax Act, in addition to introducing the Accelerated Cost Recovery System for investment in plant and equipment, introduced an incremental R&E tax credit for qualified research expenditures. Firms were eligible to claim either 25 percent credit if their R&D expenditures exceeded the average of R&D spending of the three previous years or half of the credit if they were above twice the base. This credit was initially intended to expire at the end of 1985 but was renewed at a rate of 20 percent for two additional years in the Tax Reform Act (TRA) of 1986.[6]

To estimate the effect of these two R&D tax incentives on the price of R&D, assume that a firm incurs $1 of R&D expenditures in excess of its R&D expenditures in the past three years. With an incremental tax credit of 25 percent, this means that the cost to the firm will be reduced by $1 \times 0.25 = $0.25$. However, the $1 increase in R&D expenditures decreases the incremental R&E tax credit for the next three years by $0.33 \times 0.25 = $0.083$ for each year. Thus, with a

---

[6]The credit has from then renewed at a rate of 20 percent. See Hall (1992) for a brief history of the credit rate, qualified expenditure rules and base levels during 1981-1991.

discount rate of 10 percent the net tax reduction of a $1 increase in R&D expenditures is $0.25 - [\sum_{i=1}^{3} $0.083/(1+0.10^i] = $0.045$, and the actual posttax cost of the expenditures is $1 - $0.045 = $0.955.

Consider now the effect of the immediate deductibility provision of R&D expenditures. Suppose that the corporate income tax rate is 46 percent; then the tax reduction is $0.46, and the after-tax cost of R&D expenditures $1 - $0.46 = $0.54. By combining these two incentives, the after-tax cost of $1 of R&D expenditures is $1 - $0.46 - $0.045 = $0.495 (i.e., about one-half its pretax cost).

For firms to benefit from tax incentives, they must have sufficient taxable income. In addition, in the case of incremental R&E tax credit, Eisner et al. (1984) have estimated that in 1981 and 1982, about 25 and 35 percent, respectively, of manufacturing firms did not claim the credit either because they did not increase their R&D expenditures over the base or because they did not have sufficient federal income tax liabilities. In some instances the incremental character of the credit might even make the effective rate negative (Eisner et al., 1984; Hall, 1992). In the absence of information, we assume that the firms in our sample of industries have enough tax liabilities and that the increase in their R&D expenditures was greater than the base but less than twice the base.

Under the above assumptions, let $\mu_C$ be the corporate income tax rate, $\varsigma$ the incremental R&E tax credit rate, and $\lambda$ a parameter taking values of 1 if there is immediate expensing of R&D expenditures but values less than 1 otherwise.[7] The after-tax cost of R&D expenditures is given by $q_R(1 - \lambda\mu_C - v\varsigma)$, where $q_R$ is the acquisition price, $v = [1 - \sum_{i=1}^{3} 0.33/(1+r)^i]$ and $r$ is the discount rate.[8]

Let the after-tax rental price of R&D capital services $(P_R)$ be defined by the equality between the posttax cost of acquisition and the present value of future rentals (Hall and Jorgenson, 1967). Then the posttax rental price of company-financed R&D capital is given by

$$P_R = q_R(r + \delta_R)(1 - \lambda\mu_C - v\varsigma), \tag{1}$$

where $r$ is the discount rate and $\delta_R$ is the depreciation rate of company-financed R&D capital.[9] For a given level of output, the effect of a change in R&D tax

---

[7]The parameter can be considered as the rate with which R&D expenditures are allowed to be deducted in the current period. To see the significance of immediate expensing of R&D expenditures, compare this with the case in which the government allows only that the economic depreciation of R&D expenditures be deducted from current income. The present value of the depreciation deductions of $1 of R&D with a depreciation and discount rate of 10 percent is equal to 0.50 [= 0.10/(0.10 + 0.10)], and the parameter $\lambda$ takes the value 0.50.

[8]The after-tax cost of $1 of R&D expenditures for the period 1981 to 1988 is about $0.55, where the contributions of immediate expensing and the incremental R&E tax credit are about 0.42 and 0.038, respectively. For 1981, $v = [1 - 0.5/(1+r) - \sum_{i-2}^{3} 0.33/(1+r)^i]$ since for 1982 the base was the average of R&D expenditures of 1980 and 1981 (see Eisner et al., 1984).

[9]Similar rental prices are constructed in the model for the physical capital by taking account of various taxes and subsidies that pertain to plant and equipment investment.

incentives $(T)$ on the demand for R&D capital stock and on the other inputs in industry is given by

$$\eta_{jT}^h = \partial \ln x_j^h / \partial \ln T = \varepsilon_{jR}^h (\ln p_R / \partial \ln T), \qquad T = \varsigma, \lambda, \qquad j = L, K, R, M, \qquad (2)$$

where $\varepsilon_{jR}^h$ is the price elasticity of input demands with respect to the rental price of R&D capital and $(\partial \ln p_R / \partial \ln T)$ is the elasticity of the rental price of R&D capital with respect to a change in tax incentives, which is equal to either

$$\partial \ln p_R / \partial \ln \varsigma = -v\varsigma / (1 - \lambda \mu_C - v\varsigma) \qquad (3)$$

for a change in incremental R&E credit or

$$\partial \ln p_R / \partial \ln \lambda = -\lambda \mu_C / (1 - \lambda \mu_C - v\varsigma) \qquad (4)$$

for a change in the extent of immediate expensing.

Among the empirical results from the model estimation are the following:

1. The pattern of the own-price elasticities of labor, physical capital, and intermediate inputs varies from one industry to another, whereas the own-price elasticity of company-financed R&D capital does not vary much from industry to industry. The own-price elasticity of private R&D capital ranges from −1 in textile and apparel (40), lumber, wood products and furniture (41), and other manufacturing (42) to −0.94 in scientific instruments (38). The company-financed R&D price elasticity estimated in this study is in the middle range of own-price elasticities of R&D reported in the literature. Hines (1993) has estimated a price elasticity of company-financed R&D of about −1.2; Hall (1992), about −1; whereas Nadiri and Prucha (1989) and Bernstein and Nadiri (1989) have reported a price elasticity of total R&D (company-plus publicly financed) of about −0.4 to −0.5.[10]

2. The cross-price elasticities suggest that price changes in other inputs such as labor, physical capital, and materials have significant effect on R&D investment. Company-financed R&D capital and physical capital are substitutes in most industries. It also seems that a change in the price of

---

[10]Our estimates are closer to those of Hall and Hines. The difference between our estimates of own-price elasticity of company-financed R&D and the estimates of Bernstein and Nadiri (1989) and Nadiri and Prucha (1989) can be explained by the fact that the elasticities estimated by these authors pertain to total R&D performed in industry (i.e., company-financed as well as publicly financed) and thus respond less to price changes. However, it very important to note that considerable differences in price elasticity of R&D investment could still arise due to the differences in the model specification and estimation methods.

company-financed R&D affects physical capital relatively less than a change in the price of physical capital affects company-financed R&D capital. This has the very important implication for public policy that tax measures to promote investment in structures and equipment will have significant indirect effects on R&D investment.[11]

3. Although company-financed R&D is a substitute for labor, it is a complement of intermediate inputs in low R&D-intensive industries but a weak substitute in high-technology industries such as chemicals (28), machinery (35), electrical equipment (36), transportation equipment (37), and scientific instruments (38).

In short, demand for R&D capital is affected not only by changes in its own rental prices but also by the price movements of other factors of production such as labor, physical capital, and materials. Considerable evidence from this and many other studies shows that factors of production, particularly investment in physical and R&D capital, respond to changes in after-tax prices. Our results suggest that increases in the prices of labor and physical capital lead to an increase in private R&D investment. This implies that any input price changes induced by government tax policies, whether payroll taxes, corporate taxes, or tax credits and incentives for investment in plant and equipment, will have a significant indirect effect on R&D investment. Considering R&D tax and subsidy policies in isolation from other taxes and incentives that a firm or industry faces may lead to incorrect measurement of the effects of government policies to promote R&D expenditures. Therefore, it is essential that all taxes that are levied on a firm or industry be considered together to evaluate properly the effectiveness of any R&D tax policies.

We estimated the elasticities of cost, labor, physical capital, R&D capital, and intermediate inputs with respect to incremental R&E tax credit and the rate of R&D expensing. These elasticities have been constructed by multiplying the input price elasticities by the percentage change of rental R&D price due to a change in R&D tax incentives.[12] The evidence suggests that a change in the rate of expensing has a much greater effect by far, almost 10 times, than a change in incremental R&E tax credit. This occurs because the immediate expensing of R&D expenditures constitutes 90 to 96 percent of the reduction of the cost of R&D expenditures whereas the incremental R&E tax credit is responsible for only a small fraction of the price reduction. The effect of the incremental R&E tax credit is nevertheless significant. Both effects are relatively larger in the low R&D-

---

[11]Cordes (1984), for instance, has argued that the ARCS, introduced in 1981 for plant and equipment investment, has moved the price of physical capital relative to R&D capital in favor of the former. Thus, the introduction of an incremental R&E tax credit was necessary to restore in some measure incentives for R&D investment.

[12]The elasticity of cost with respect of tax incentives is given by $\eta^h_{CT} = \partial \ln C^h / \partial \ln T = S^h_R (\partial \ln p^h_R / \partial \ln T)$.

intensive industries than in high-technology industries, reflecting the fact that industries with a long tradition of R&D investment respond less to the cost changes of R&D investment. This is consistent with the evidence from the tax forms of 1981, 1982 and 1983 (see Cordes (1988, 1989) showing that after the introduction of R&E tax credit, the high-technology manufacturing industries reported smaller increases in R&D expenditures than other manufacturing industries.

Based on the model estimates, the incremental R&E tax credit generated, on average, about $2.5 billion dollars of additional R&D expenditures per year in the manufacturing sector during 1981-1988. If it is adjusted with the eligibility ratio of about 0.63 (see Eisner et al., 1984), the R&E credit has stimulated about $1.6 billion dollars of additional R&D expenditures per year.[13] This estimate is consistent with those reported by Baily and Lawrence (1992), Hall (1992), and Hines (1993), although it may be biased upward because there is evidence that many firms redefined activities as R&D after the introduction of the R&E credit.

Suppose that the government, instead of allowing the immediate deductibility of R&D investment, allows only the economic depreciation of R&D expenditures to be deducted from current income. With a discount rate and depreciation rate of 10 percent (see footnote 6), this implies that the value of the parameter $\lambda$ is 0.5 and will account for, on average, about 35 percent decline in R&D expenditures, or about $16 billion per year for the manufacturing sector as a whole. Disallowing immediate deductibility of R&D expenditures would have much greater negative impact on R&D expenditures than abolishing the R&E tax credit. Production costs would rise by $14.3 billion as a result of the removal of 100 percent deductibility and by $2.6 billion as a result of abolishing tax credit. Industry-financed R&D would be reduced by similar magnitudes, $13.7 billion and $2.5 billion, respectively, with greatest impact falling on R&D-intensive industries (28, 35, 36, 37, and 38). The combined contribution of the tax credit and immediate deductibility of R&D expenditures is about $18 billion per year of additional R&D expenditures. This amounts to approximately 40 percent of the total privately financed R&D of the entire manufacturing sector. Moreover, if one takes into account the fact that government directly finances about 30 percent of total R&D performed in the manufacturing sector, the role of the federal government in support of R&D is quite clear.

## EFFECTIVENESS OF R&D TAX POLICY

One way to evaluate the effectiveness of R&D tax policies is to measure the additional private R&D expenditures generated by the tax policies relative to forgone tax revenues. There is some disagreement among economists about the

---

[13]Cordes (1989) has estimated that the credit stimulated about $560 million to $1.5 billion, whereas Hall (1992) has estimated that the additional spending stimulated is about $2 billion 1982 dollars per year.

effectiveness of R&E tax credit. For instance, Mansfield (1984, 1986) has estimated that the additional R&D expenditure per dollar cost to the government
ranges between 0.3 and 0.4. Baily and Lawrence (1992) have estimated it to be
about 1 to 1.3. About the same estimates as Baily's are provided by Hines (1993),
whereas Hall (1992) estimates that the ratio is about 2. These differences in estimates are basically due to the differences in price elasticities of R&D estimated
by the authors.

Our estimate suggests, on average, a benefit-cost ratio of R&E tax credit of
about 0.95 for the period 1981 to 1988 for industries included in the sample. If
this ratio is compared with the findings reported by other studies, our estimate is
in the middle range. From our analysis, we can conclude that the R&E tax credit
has not been a failure as the early literature on the subject had suggested, but
rather that it has had a modest impact in stimulating private R&D investment.
Moreover, if one takes into account the induced output effect from increases in
industry R&D expenditures, as well as the spillovers from such investments, then
the benefit-cost ratio of the incremental R&E credit will be higher.[14]

Table 3.2 reports the results of the following experiment. Assume that for
the year 1988 the government abolishes the incremental R&E tax credit and allows only the economic depreciation of R&D expenditures to be deducted from
the current income. With these assumptions, our estimates imply that the additional cost for the industry of the revenues saved by the government would be
about $16.9 billion, but the reduction of R&D tax incentives in turn increases the
rental price of company-financed R&D, leading to a reduction of $16.2 billion in
private R&D investment.

The cost increases and reductions in R&D investment are not uniform across
industries. In fact, in R&D-intensive industries, costs will rise as a consequence
of the change in public R&D policy. However, the cost increases and reduction in
R&D investment in response to the hypothesized changes in R&D tax policies
are very large in R&D-intensive industries such as chemicals (28), machinery
(35), electrical equipment (36), and transportation equipment (37). Low-technology industries, such as food and kindred products (20) and other manufacturers
(42), would not be affected as much. This, of course, is not surprising because in
the low-technology industries, R&D cost shares are very small; thus, removal of
the subsidies has a relatively smaller effect on their cost.

The results reported in the two previous sections are based on the pre-1988
structure of the R&E credit. However, a recent extension of the analysis to the
post-1988 period suggests that these observations also hold for the year 1992.
The magnitudes of the effects vary over time and across industries, but the general policy conclusions remain the same.

---

[14]For the empirical literature that supports this hypothesis, see Nadiri (1993).

**TABLE 3.2**   Effect of R&D Tax Incentives on Production Cost and Demand for Private R&D in Manufacturing Industries in 1988 (in billions of current dollars)

| Industry Code | Zero R&E Tax Credit (from 20%) (A) | | 10% R&D Depreciation Rate (from 100%) (B) | | Effect of Removing R&D Tax Incentives (A) + (B) | |
|---|---|---|---|---|---|---|
| | Cost | R&D Capital | Cost | R&D Capital | Cost | R&D Capital |
| 20 | 0.05 | –0.05 | 0.26 | –0.26 | 0.31 | –0.30 |
| 26 | 0.03 | –0.03 | 0.19 | –0.18 | 0.22 | –0.22 |
| 28 | 0.42 | –0.40 | 2.32 | –2.22 | 2.74 | –2.62 |
| 29 | 0.11 | –0.11 | 0.60 | –0.59 | 0.71 | –0.70 |
| 30 | 0.04 | –0.04 | 0.22 | –0.21 | 0.26 | –0.25 |
| 32 | 0.04 | –0.04 | 0.21 | –0.21 | 0.25 | –0.25 |
| 33 | 0.05 | –0.04 | 0.25 | –0.24 | 0.29 | –0.29 |
| 34 | 0.04 | –0.04 | 0.22 | –0.22 | 0.26 | –0.26 |
| 35 | 0.47 | –0.45 | 2.59 | –2.49 | 3.06 | –2.94 |
| 36 | 0.47 | –0.45 | 2.62 | –2.47 | 3.10 | –2.92 |
| 37 | 0.61 | –0.59 | 3.38 | –3.25 | 4.00 | –3.83 |
| 38 | 0.21 | –0.20 | 1.16 | –1.09 | 1.37 | –1.28 |
| 40 | 0.03 | –0.03 | 0.18 | –0.18 | 0.21 | –0.21 |
| 41 | 0.01 | –0.01 | 0.06 | –0.06 | 0.07 | –0.07 |
| 42 | 0.01 | –0.01 | 0.05 | –0.05 | 0.06 | –0.06 |
| Total | 2.6 | –2.5 | 14.3 | –13.7 | 16.9 | –16.2 |

## R&E CREDIT: POSSIBLE IMPROVEMENTS

The extensive literature evaluating the effectiveness of R&E credit[15] is beyond the scope of this chapter to survey. I can outline, however, a few criticisms and the benefits of potential improvements in the effectiveness of this fiscal instrument.

The current R&E credit is not targeted sufficiently to be very effective. For example, different types of R&D with different types of productivity and social rates of return may require a more flexible approach. In addition, the tax credits it is often claimed, accrue mainly to large firms in a few industries. Some of these, for example, defense contractors, are also major recipients of public R&D expenditures. A more flexible and targeted tax would be less vulnerable to these criticisms. For example, the credit could be focused to promote basic research and encourage university-industry cooperation in fields of research and development.

The mechanics of qualifying an R&D project, establishing the base year, and

---

[15]See Hall (1992, 1995) for an extensive review of the history, methodological issues, and regulations pertaining to the R&E tax credit in the United States and other Organization for Economic Cooperation and Development (OECD) countries. Also see Office of Technology Assessment (1996) and OECD (1996).

classifying R&D expenses are not trivial challenges. An effort to simplify and tighten the existing rules is a worthwhile undertaking.

The on-again, off-again history of the R&E credit has contributed to great uncertainty on the part of firms and may have undermined the stimulus to R&D investment. Because of these and other problems associated with the law, administrative costs entailed with the R&E credit are high.[16] The benefits of R&E credit would be significantly greater if it were permanent.

There is a need for R&D tax policies to promote not only new investment in knowledge creation but also dissemination of existing knowledge and findings among enterprises and industries. Small businesses, public-sector organizations, and traditionally low R&D-intensive sectors would benefit from a well-targeted technology diffusion policy.

There are two fundamental problems, one theoretical and the other practical, in evaluating the results of the econometric evidence and other methods to ascertain the effectiveness of the R&E tax credit:

1. The theoretical issue arises from the fact that firms may undertake R&D investment in part for strategic and competitive reasons. To that extent, they are likely to invest in R&D regardless of R&D tax treatment, although they will certainly have a financial interest in claiming the tax credit.
2. The measurement problem is related to the unsatisfactory state of the R&D price deflator used in various studies. There has been some effort to improve the quality of these deflators at both the aggregate and the firm levels, but the results are not satisfactory.

## CONCLUSION

We have examined the effects of R&D tax policy on the cost structure of the manufacturing industries. It is important to recognize that R&D-specific tax measures are just part of a much larger set of taxes and governmental, fiscal policies that firms face at a given period. Firms rearrange their demand for various inputs to minimize their costs, taking into account the entire set of taxes that they may face. Firms' demands for inputs, particularly investments in physical and R&D capital, respond to changes in their own rental prices as well as to the price changes of other inputs. The cross-price effects can be large and significant. For example, in our study, an increase in the rental price of physical capital or the price of labor induces firms to invest more in R&D.

The existing R&E tax credit has been at best a modest success. The evidence on its cost-effectiveness is not as weak as to warrant abolishing it all together.[17]

---

[16]See Hall (1995) for further discussion.
[17]See Mansfield (1986).

The immediate deductibility of R&D expenditures is by far the more important subsidy. If the government switched treating R&D expenditures like tangible investments, there would be a substantial reduction of privately financed R&D investment. As shown elsewhere, it seems that publicly financed R&D investment is a more appropriate tool for increasing efficiency and possibly for stimulating output growth, whereas R&D tax policy is a more appropriate tool for stimulating private-sector R&D investment.[18] Using data for 1957-1992, our recent analysis suggests that the results reported here also hold for the years immediately following 1988.

Both instruments, subsidies and direct financing of publicly financed R&D expenditures, are important means of sustaining balanced output and productivity growth in the manufacturing sector, but current R&D tax policy should be reexamined to increase its effectiveness in promoting private investment in technological innovation diffusion.

## ACKNOWLEDGMENT

The support from C.V. Starr Center for Applied Economics of New York University is gratefully acknowledged. I would also like to thank Seongjun Kim and Frances Hui for their help.

## REFERENCES

Arrow, K.J. 1962. "Economic welfare and the allocations of resources for invention." In *The Rate and Direction of Inventive Activity: Economic and Social Factors*, R. Nelson, ed. National Bureau of Economic Research. Princeton: Princeton University Press.

Baily, M.N., and R.Z. Lawrence. 1992. *Tax Incentives for R&D: What Do the Data Tell Us?* Study commissioned by the Council on Research and Technology, Washington, D.C.

Bernstein, J. 1986. *Research and Development, Tax Incentives and the Structure of Production and Financing.* Toronto: University of Toronto Press.

Bernstein, J., and M.I. Nadiri. 1989. "Rates of return on physical and R&D capital and structure of production process: Cross section and time series evidence." In *Advances in Econometrics and Modeling*, B. Raj, ed. Dordrecht: the Netherlands: Kluwer.

Carmichael, J. 1981. "The effects of mission-oriented public R&D spending on private industry." *Journal of Finance* 36:617-627.

Cohen, W.M., and R.C. Levin. 1989. "Empirical studies of innovation and market structure." In *Handbook of Inudstrial Organization, Vol. II*, R. Scmalenses and R.D. Willing, eds., New York: North Holland.

Cordes, J.J. 1984. "R&D tax incentives." In *The R&E Tax Credit: Issues in Tax Policy and Industrial Innovations*, K. Brown, ed. Washington, D.C.: American Enterprise Institute for Public Policy.

Cordes, J.J. 1988. "The impact of tax policy on the creation of new technical knowledge: An assessment of the evidence." In *The Effect of Technological Change on Employment and Economic Growth*, R. Cyert and D. Mawrey, eds. Cambridge, Mass.: Ballinger.

---

[18]See Mamuneas and Nadiri (1996).

Cordes, J.J. 1989. "Tax incentives and R&D spending: A review of the evidence." *Research Policy* 18:119-133.

Eisner, R., S. Albert, and M.A. Sullivan. 1984. "The new incremental tax credit for R&D: Incentive or disincentive?" *National Tax Journal* (June)37:171-183.

Griliches, Z. 1979. "Issues in assessing the contribution of research and development to productivity growth." *Bell Journal of Economics* 10(1):92-116.

Griliches, Z. 1991. *The Search for R&D Spillovers.* Working paper no. 3768. Cambridge, Mass: National Bureau of Economic Research.

Hall, B.H. 1992. "R&D tax policy during the eighties: Success or failure?" Paper prepared for the National Bureau of Economic Research Tax Policy Conference. Washington, D.C.

Hall, B.H. 1995. "Effectiveness of research and experiment tax credits: Critical literature review and research design." Report for the Office of Technology Assessment, U.S. Congress. Washington, D.C.

Hall, B.H., and D. Jorgenson. 1967. "Tax policy and investment behavior." *American Economic Review* 57:391-414.

Hines, J.R. 1993. "On the sensitivity of R&D to delicate tax changes: The behavior of U.S. multinationals in the 1980s." In *Studies in International Taxation,* A. Giovannini, R.G. Hubbard, and J. Slemrod, eds. Chicago: University of Chicago Press.

Levy, D.M., and N.E. Terleckyj. 1983. "Effects of government R&D on private R&D investment and productivity: A macroeconomics analysis." *Bell Journal of Economics* 14(2).

Lichtenberg, F.R. 1988. "The private R&D investment response to federal design and technological competitions." *American Economic Review* 78:550-559.

Mamuneas, T.P., and M.I. Nadiri. 1996. "Public R&D policies and cost behavior of the U.S. manufacturing industries." *Journal of Public Economics* 63:57-81.

Mansfield, E. 1984. *Public Policy Toward Industrial Innovation: An International Study of Direct Tax Incentives for R&D.* Presented at the 75th Anniversary Colloquium on Productivity and Technology. Cambridge, Mass.: Harvard Business School.

Mansfield, E. 1986. "The R&D tax credit and other technology policy issues." *American Economic Review* 76(2):190-194.

Mohnen, P. 1990. "Relationship between R&D and productivity growth in Canada and other major industrialized countries." Report of the Economic Council of Canada.

Nadiri, M.I. 1993. *Innovations and Technological Spillovers.* Working paper no. 4423. Cambridge, Mass.: National Bureau of Economic Research.

Nadiri, M.I., and I.R. Prucha. 1989. *Dynamic Factor Demand Models, Productivity Measurement, and Rates of Return: Theory and an Empirical Application to the U.S. Bell System.* Working paper no. 3041. Cambridge, Mass.: National Bureau of Economic Research.

Organization for Economic Cooperation and Development. 1996. *Fiscal Measures to Promote R&D and Innovation.* Paris: OECD.

Romer, P. 1990. "Are nonconvexities important for understanding growth?" *American Economic Review* 80(2): 97-103.

Spence, M. 1984. "Cost-reduction, competition and industry performance." *Econometrica* 52(1):101-121.

U.S. Congress, Office of Technology Assessment. 1996. *The Effectiveness of Research and Experimentation Tax Credits.* Washington, D.C.: U.S. Government Printing Office.

# 4

# International Tax Policy, Investment, and Technology[1]

HARRY GRUBERT
*U. S. Department of the Treasury*

## MEASUREMENT OF NET INCOME

Although allocation rules may seem arbitrary and a nuisance, they arise out of the necessity, under an income tax, to measure net foreign income. Countries such as the United States that allow a credit for foreign income tax limit the credit to what the home country tax would be on the income. Otherwise, there would be an incentive for foreign governments to raise their taxes and effectively collect revenue on domestic U.S. income. Net foreign income, therefore, has to be measured. The problem is even more acute under an exemption or territorial system in which (active) foreign income is exempt from home-country tax. Any increased allocation of expenses to foreign income directly increases home-country tax liability.

The problem of allocating overhead expenses is familiar to us all as personal taxpayers and is motivated by considerations similar to those that give rise to expense allocations to foreign income. Many members of the academic community are probably acquainted with the "home office" deduction in which housing expenses have to be allocated between business and nonbusiness uses. Investment in tax-exempt state and local bonds is an example in which interest expenses have to be divided between taxable and non-taxable income. If an individual borrows and invests in state and local bonds, the Internal Revenue Code may limit the amount of deductible interest expense. This is analogous to a company that borrows at home and invests abroad where the income might be deferred indefinitely or, in any case, be out of the home-country tax base because it is shielded by foreign tax credits.

---

[1]Nothing in these remarks should be construed as reflecting the view of the U.S. Treasury Department.

## 1995 REGULATIONS FOR R&D ALLOCATIONS

Jim Hines describes in his chapter the R&D allocation regulations, issued in 1995, that supersede the substantially more onerous regulations originally promulgated in 1977. I would like to add a few observations to put them in perspective. Consider a U.S. company that performs domestic R&D and, using the results of its ongoing R&D program, has foreign sales just equal to its domestic sales. Then, if it can take full advantage of the "optional gross income method" in the regulations, which is apparently very common, the company will allocate 12.5 percent of its R&D expenses to foreign income.[2] In other words, the allocation to domestic income is seven times the allocation to foreign income even though foreign and domestic sales are equal.

Furthermore, because of the royalty rule that Hines mentions, the U.S. tax regime for high-technology companies is much more favorable than the regime faced by comparable foreign companies based in an exemption country. For example, Germany exempts the active foreign income of its companies by treaty, but this territorial exemption does not generally extend to royalties, which are fully taxable. In contrast, a U.S.-based multinational corporation (MNC) in an excess foreign tax credit position would earn royalties that are both deductible from foreign tax and free from U.S. tax while losing only a relatively small part of its R&D deductions through allocations to foreign income.

## HOW MUCH U.S. R&D IS ALLOCATED TO FOREIGN INCOME?

U.S. companies now report their R&D allocations on the tax form on which they calculate their foreign tax credit. In addition to the optional gross income method mentioned earlier, there are several reasons why allocations seem to be smaller than a straightforward application of the sales method would suggest. Companies can exclude "legally mandated R&D" that cannot be expected to have value abroad. Testing required by the Food and Drug Administration is cited in the regulations as an example. Foreign sales are to be taken into account only if the foreign affiliate "can reasonably be expected to benefit directly or indirectly from the taxpayer's research expense connected with the product category." Also, foreign sales do not attract an allocation if the foreign affiliate has entered into a "bona fide" cost-sharing arrangement with the parent U.S. company. The evidence on actual allocations suggests that companies allocate only about one-half

---

[2]Under the sales method, companies first allocate 50 percent of R&D exclusively to domestic income and the remainder to foreign and domestic income based on sales. The sales method would, therefore, allocate 25 percent ($0.5 \times 0.5$) to foreign income. Under the optional gross income method, the allocation to foreign income can be reduced to the greater of *half* of the sales allocation or the pure gross income allocation. Foreign *gross* income tends to be low relative to domestic gross income because it is made up largely of (repatriated) net income items such as dividends and royalties and does not include depreciation, interest, and other overhead expenses that are in domestic gross income.

of the U.S. R&D to foreign income that Jim Hines estimates in his studies. He may, therefore, be substantially overstating the impact of the allocation rules.

## RESIDUAL U.S. TAX RATE ON FOREIGN BUSINESS INCOME

To assess the significance of the international tax rules, it is useful to look at the residual U.S. tax rate on foreign business income and how it has changed since the Tax Reform Act of 1986. In 1984, the residual U.S. tax rate on the foreign income earned by U.S. manufacturing companies in the "general" or active basket was 8 percent. By 1992, primarily as a result of the large drop in the statutory corporate tax rate in the Tax Reform Act (TRA) of 1986, the residual U.S. tax on active foreign income had fallen to about 4 percent. Even if we adjust for other provisions of the TRA, including the financial services income basket, the baskets of "10 to 50 percent owned" companies, and the expansion of the passive basket, the residual rate still seems to be substantially lower than it was in 1984. Accordingly, the complaints, perhaps justified, by the business community about changes in the international tax system brought about by the TRA must reflect the greater complexity of the new rules and their effect on domestic business decisions, not any increase in tax burdens.

Furthermore, these estimates of residual U.S. tax are based on foreign-source income and expense as defined in the tax code, which may not give a true picture of income and tax burdens on actual foreign operations. For example, the foreign income base does not include income earned by foreign affiliates that is not currently repatriated. Also, some of the income identified as foreign source actually arises from domestic operations. For example, 50 percent of export sales income can be classified as foreign source and absorb excess foreign tax credits generated by operations abroad. To that extent, the international tax system provides a bonus for foreign operations. If a company has excess foreign tax credits, not only is there no residual U.S. tax but some of the foreign tax credits can offset the U.S. tax on domestic operations. On the other hand, in some cases, foreign income can be understated, for example, because allocations of interest expenses may be higher than they would be under the more conceptually correct "worldwide fungibility." Grubert and Mutti (1995) make various adjustments for understatements and overstatements and conclude that the residual U.S. tax rate on operating income abroad is very small and, indeed, might even be negative.

## RESPONSIVENESS OF INVESTMENT LOCATION
## TO LOCAL TAX RATES

Joel Slemrod has mentioned my recent paper with Jack Mutti on taxes and the location of investment (Grubert and Mutti, 1996), giving me the opportunity to elaborate on it further. Our paper used the 1992 Treasury Department tax files to study the investment choices of more than 500 large U.S. manufacturing companies in 60 potential foreign locations. The choice of investment location abroad seems very responsive to the local effective tax rate. After combining both the decision to locate in a foreign country and the decision about how much to invest there, we concluded that the overall elasticity of capital with respect to the change in $1 - t$ (i.e., one minus the tax rate; or the change in the after-tax rate of return given the pretax return) is about three.

Another way of evaluating the importance of local tax rates is to use the results to estimate the extent to which the distribution of real capital among the 60 foreign locations would be altered if taxes did not play a role. We concluded that about 15 percent of the U.S. manufacturing capital abroad would be in a different foreign location but for the effect of taxes.. We were surprised by the influence attributed to taxes, but the specific pattern of the results tended to strengthen our confidence. For example, investments by electronics and computer companies seem much more sensitive to taxes than those of companies in foods and pharmaceuticals, in which local market and regulatory considerations are more likely to be dominant. Also, production for sale to other foreign affiliates appears to be especially sensitive to local tax rates, which seems plausible.

Still, Jack Mutti and I continue to worry that we have overestimated the importance of taxes. It was, therefore, interesting to hear from the business participants at this conference that their operations have become very mobile. The growth of the "virtual corporation," "flexible" work forces, and the importance of new attractive locations with low tax rates suggest that perhaps we were not far off the mark.

Yet we should be clear that no inferences can be drawn from our results about the role of taxes in the choice between the United States and potential foreign locations. The distribution of U.S. capital among foreign locations was the subject. The only evidence we presented on the U.S.-versus-foreign choice was that there seemed to be no relationship between the tax sensitivity of an industry and the share of its capital that was abroad.

Finally, my colleagues and I are planning to link the 1984, 1992, and perhaps 1994 files to study the changes in location over the period. This, we believe, has several advantages. It covers the period of the Tax Reform Act of 1986, which altered the incentive to invest in various locations. The response of location to changes in tax rates also makes it possible to control for fixed geographical effects that are difficult to identify in a single cross section. Another advantage is that the TRA changed the effective tax rates on investment in the United States by varying amounts in different industries, so it may be possible to identify the role of taxes in the choice between U.S. and foreign locations.

## REFERENCES

Grubert, H., and J. Mutti. 1995. "Taxing multinationals in a world with portfolio flows and R&D: Is capital export neutrality absolute?" *International Tax and Public Finance* 2:439-457.

Grubert, H., and J. Mutti. 1996. "Do Taxes Influence Where U.S. Corporations Invest?," prepared for presentation at the Conference of the Trans-Atlantic Public Economics Seminar, Amsterdam.

# II

## INDUSTRY PERSPECTIVES ON THE IMPACT OF INTERNATIONAL TAX RULES

# 5

# Impact of Tax Incentives on the Location of Investment: A Corporate Perspective

PETER E. NUGENT
*Merck & Co., Inc.*

## MAGNITUDE AND DURATION OF TAX INCENTIVES

A multinational's decision to locate an investment in a particular country is generally based on all relevant economic, operational, and financial factors. Taxation is only one of these factors. The tremendous impact of section 936 of the Internal Revenue Code on the economy of Puerto Rico is clear evidence that a substantial tax benefit can dramatically influence the location of investment. The impact of more modest tax incentives is far more difficult to assess.

I have never seen a minor tax benefit tip the scale in a major investment decision. Uncertainty about future tax law changes discounts the value of favorable tax regimes, often to the point that the perceived tax cost differential between locations is overwhelmed by the intuitive preferences of operating management. A tax incentive under constant threat of repeal or one that will expire unless extended by legislation must be far greater than a permanent incentive if it is to have the same influence on corporate decision making.

## LOCATION OF RESEARCH AND DEVELOPMENT

Recent developments in communication and information technology have made the geographic dispersal of R&D activities substantially more feasible than it was just 10 years ago. E-mail, teleconferencing, and electronic global information repositories have facilitated the management and coordination of R&D projects at great distances. Thus, geographic proximity, which used to be a dominant factor in decisions to locate R&D, has diminished in importance As a consequence, tax considerations have increased in relative importance.

There is a spectrum of R&D location decisions. At one end is the decision to locate a major capital investment in a new world-class basic research facility. At the other end is the decision to locate more routine research activities. Often this type of activity is a recurring component of a broad class of R&D projects. In many cases, these activities can be assigned readily to any one of a number of proficient internal or external facilities.

The first type of decision has far-reaching consequences and will be governed by a long-term assessment of productivity drivers, such as the ability to recruit top scientific talent, the estimated capital investment, and projected operating costs. This decision may also be influenced by collateral business objectives such as enhancement of the company's presence in an important market. In certain cases, the long-term political and economic stability of the country will be an issue. When making a choice between developed countries, tax is often a relatively unimportant factor in this type of decision.

The second type of decision is generally a simple matter of cost, quality, and delivery date and may also involve conventional staffing and resource allocation considerations. It is at this end of the spectrum that R&D activities become relatively portable and more readily influenced by tax incentives.

A tax incentive that influences decisions of the first type will usually have a greater and more lasting effect on the economy. Trying to influence these decisions with minor, temporary tax incentives is just wishful thinking. On the other hand, a U.S. multinational in a perpetual excess foreign tax credit position might very well locate a new world-class basic research facility outside the United States to avoid the unfavorable consequences of Treasury Department Regulations section 861-17 (allocation and apportionment of research and experimental expenditures)[1]. The adverse consequences of the 861-8 regime for a U.S. multinational with a substantial foreign presence are rarely minor, and accordingly, the company's forecast of its foreign tax credit position is likely to be the critical factor in evaluating the cost of a U.S. location.

## CONSEQUENCES OF COMPLEXITY

Tax incentives and disincentives for investment are often unintentional. The international provisions of the U.S. Internal Revenue Code have become so complex that the architects who regularly patch up this structure may fail to perceive the behavioral consequences of new layers of complexity. The enactment and repeal of section 956A of the Internal Revenue Code, an anti-deferral provision, is one example. Another, less obvious, example is section 904(g). This provision of the Internal Revenue Code was originally intended to curtail the use of a for-

---

[1]The allocation and apportionment of research and experimental expenditures were formerly governed by Treasury Department Regulations section 861-8 and the issues arising under these regulations continue to be identified by references to "861-8".

eign subsidiary to shift the source of income from domestic to foreign, thereby increasing the capacity of the U.S. parent to credit foreign taxes. Under section 904(g) if 10 percent or more of the earnings of a foreign subsidiary are derived from sources within the United States, a ratable portion of dividends paid by the subsidiary is treated as domestic source income. The apparent motivation for the enactment of section 904(g) was to shut down schemes involving portable income in tax havens. In its current form, however, it applies broadly to all sorts of income no matter how legitimately or heavily taxed by foreign governments.

Unintended consequences arise when a foreign subsidiary operating in a high-tax country discovers and develops a blockbuster product through its own R&D program. The income from global exploitation of this product may dwarf the level of income historically reported by the subsidiary. Given the relative importance of the U.S. market, it is assumed for purposes of this example that if the subsidiary were to license the manufacture of the product in the United States to its U.S. parent (even for U.S. market requirements only), the U.S. source royalty income received by the subsidiary would exceed 10 percent of its earnings.

If the U.S. parent is in an excess foreign tax credit position, there will be a double tax on the U.S. source royalty paid to the subsidiary—once when the subsidiary pays tax in its home country and again in the United States when the subsidiary's earnings are distributed to the U.S. parent. There are various ways to solve this problem but none of them involves manufacturing in the United States. So for this company there are two disincentives to invest in the United States—a disincentive to locate R&D in the United States under the 861-8 regime and later, when its overseas R&D generates a product, a disincentive to manufacture the product in the United States.

Carrying on research in a foreign subsidiary is not a tax abuse, and neither is the payment of a royalty to the foreign owner of a U.S. patent. These are normal business activities caught in a web of tax provisions so complex that in some cases, no one can confidently predict the economic behavior that will result from the latest attempt to "plug a leak."

# 6

# The Virtual Global Electronic Economy

ROBERT N. MATTSON
*IBM Corporation*

Global business enterprises in the next century will be borderless organizations built around information networks, flexible work forces, and webs of strategic alliances. In this environment, current U.S. tax policy on international investment is outmoded. Economic conditions have changed dramatically since the U.S. tax rules controlling international operations were adopted 35 years ago. The U.S. economy's percentage of the world gross domestic product (GDP) is half of what it was 30 years ago. U.S. exports of high-technology goods relative to those of other OECD (Organization for Economic Cooperation and Development) member countries dropped by 40 percent during this period. U.S. outward direct investment in 1960 was five times inward investment, today, the flows are about equal (Hufbauer, 1992, Table 1.1).

Before we can analyze the impact of U.S. tax policy on international investment, it is necessary to understand three major fundamental changes in the global business environment—(1) globalization, (2) quantum leaps in technology, and (3) the emergence of a new set of technologically skilled nations. Unfortunately, none of these changes has ever been considered in the numerous recent piecemeal changes in U.S. tax law affecting international business.

## GLOBALIZATION

Businesses no longer can focus solely on geographical borders. Many large global companies have increasingly integrated their regional business activities. It is not uncommon that they conduct their businesses at a Pan-European, Pan-American (especially after NAFTA [the North American Free Trade Agreement]), or Pan-Asian level.

Globalization involves R&D, manufacturing, and the marketing of goods, services, and know-how on a worldwide level so that geographic boundaries become only impediments. In the past, value was determined by the tangible goods manufactured in plants located where comparative advantage dictated and the inputs of capital and labor could be employed.

In the twenty-first century, know-how, ideas, and concepts—intangible goods—will drive economic value. The nature of manufacturing in the coming era of information and high-intangible technologies will, of necessity, require governments to rethink tax policy. In contrast to the past, when know-how needed to be dispersed and duplicated at each plant location, globalization will lead to its centralization and distribution by networks. A contract manufacturing model with widely dispersed assembled work forces will be cost-effective with centralized know-how. At the same time, networks of integrated R&D laboratories have renewed the interest in cost-sharing arrangements. Governments naturally fear erosion of their tax base and have not understood this new environment.

Globalization is probably best represented by the emerging virtual corporation. This is the way in which U.S. global companies and their foreign competitors will operate in the future. These agile entities will have a quick response capability linked by electronic mail and data exchange. Their manufacturing units will operate with CAD (computer-aided design) system linkages and will have portable videoconferencing capability via laptop computer connections.

## QUANTUM LEAPS IN TECHNOLOGY

New technologies such as the Internet should not cause governments to enact special tax regimes or to add electronic "tollbooths." These technologies are progressions of older communications and knowledge delivery systems such as the telephone, radio, television, and cable. As electronic commerce evolves, it will undoubtedly be the most significant contributor to the growth of U.S. exports in the next century.

Transactions in intangible goods (e.g., software), information, and services can be accommodated within the tax compliance systems existing today. This requires great vigilance to prevent such tollbooth taxes as a recently discussed "bit tax" on the digital "bit" stream over computer telecom, cable, and satellite proposed by a member of the European Commission's High Level Expert Group on the Social and Societal Aspects of the Information Society (Soete, 1996). The "bit" tax would probably be the most complex tariff ever devised, requiring significant technical resources to implement, monitor, and audit and distorting flows of information dramatically in ways that cannot be foreseen.

Product cycles and time to market are no longer measured in calendar years but in "web" years (three-month lapse time). Collaborative R&D at labs in numerous time zones on a global basis is the new virtual model for conducting research and development projects in the corporation of the twenty-first century.

The virtual corporation's units are linked by a new information technology. Supplier and customers are now included in product design, quality assurance, packaging decisions, and other formerly confidential internal processes. The telecommunications, cable, television, computer, and energy (electric utilities) industries are converging into a network-centric business environment.

A static tax code, based on restrictive "source" tax rules and including limitations on foreign tax credits resulting in double tax barriers, will only constrain investment and high-paying job creation. Information technologies are not just about making business better, they are about making business possible.

## EMERGING TECHNOLOGICAL NATIONS

Hungry for capital investment and offering the virtual corporation low or tax-free zones, newly developed nations are providing well-trained work forces with low labor rates. As these nations improve their educational and productive opportunities, high rates of growth will emerge. Southeast Asia and Eastern Europe, which offer such assembled work forces, will be attractive to manufacturing and R&D investments in the era of information networks. Rapid, intangible technology transfer to almost any place on the globe will be possible with these new technologies.

These nations will offer advantages for joint venture alliances where few companies wish to bear the entire risk of such investments, for example, multi-billion-dollar semiconductor factories, which are being located in countries previously considered unreliable for this type of investment. U.S. international tax rules relating to joint venture alliances are equally outmoded and constitute barriers to the way business is conducted. U.S. tax rules penalize foreign joint ventures of U.S. global enterprises by fractionalizing the foreign tax credit rules with separate "baskets" for each venture.

## CHANGING TAX LANDSCAPE

It is heartening to observe the hands-off policy of the U.S. government in its review of electronic commerce and the internet (Department of the Treasury, 1996):[1]

> These technologies present tremendous opportunities to enrich all of our lives in so many ways, many of which we are likely not to have envisioned . . . Some have even speculated that the traditional corporation could itself become obsolete in certain cases as "virtual corporations" bring together varying groups of consultant and independent contractors on a project-by-project basis.

---

[1]A more problematic position is reflected in a discussion note submitted to the OECD Committee on Fiscal Affairs by representatives of the United States, Canada, and Australia in June 1996. It expressed concern about potential erosion of the tax base because of the increased international mobility of services and capital.

One of the greatest impediments to the new global business model is a set of vastly complex rules enacted in 1962. These rules were unnecessarily made even more restrictive in the 1986 Tax Reform Act. Subpart F of the Internal Revenue Code, sections 951-964, was aimed at preventing U.S. multinational companies from establishing "controlled foreign corporations" (foreign subsidiaries) in tax havens where they conducted little or no business but "squirreled away" large sums of money. The income of foreign subsidiaries is generally taxed at source, and a residual U.S. tax applies when the earnings are repatriated to the United States. U.S. tax is generally "deferred" until repatriation. Under the credit system for foreign taxes paid at the source of the earnings, U.S. tax arises only when the foreign effective tax rate is lower than the U.S. corporate tax rate of 35 percent, and then only on the residual at the time of repatriation.

Today the U.S. corporate tax rate is high, especially when one considers the double taxation of corporate earnings, which most developed countries have eliminated. Many countries, including the United Kingdom and Sweden, have sharply lower tax rates. Emerging technologically developed nations in Asia and Eastern Europe offer low labor and tax rates with educated work forces. They have attracted investments from many global corporations throughout the world. A great deal of active cross-border sales and services between these centers is now subject to these subpart F rules in the U.S. tax law. These are active business investments that were never intended to be penalized by the anti-deferral rules of subpart F. Nevertheless, these outmoded U.S. tax rules have raised the tax hurdles on U.S. global companies and interfered with business investment decisions.

Reforming the international rules under U.S. tax laws is urgently needed.[2] The emergence of virtual corporations undertaking active business investment in newly technological nations linked by information technologies and conducting electronic commerce heightens this urgency. High-tax countries such as Germany, Italy, and Japan will by necessity have to deal with the "hollowing out" of their investment base as the decreasing emphasis on boundaries leads to offshore joint investments. Germany and Italy have just announced tax reform measures to reduce their corporate taxes. Unfortunately, the United States is now arguably among high-tax countries. The total income tax burden in the United States is nearly 40 percent, including state income taxes.

In the twenty-first century, strategic investments will not be made in high-tax countries. We will have to focus U.S. tax policy on lowering hurdles, barriers, and impediments to U.S. corporations competing in the global marketplace.

---

[2]The Taxpayer Relief Act of 1997 took a small step toward such reform but much more is needed to secure the competitiveness of American-owned businesses. For example, a proposal to eliminate punative subpart F treatment of cross-border business transactions within the European Union was not enacted.

# REFERENCES

Hufbauer, G.C. 1992. *U.S. Taxation of International Income: Blueprint for Reform.* Institute for International Economics. Washington, D.C.

Soete, L. 1996. Interim Report. European Union: January.

U.S. Department of the Treasury, Office of Tax Policy. 1996. Selected Tax Policy Implications of Global Electronic Commerce. Washington, D.C.: U.S. Government Printing Office.

# 7

# Operating Through Joint Ventures Under U.S. International Tax Rules: Global Competition for R&D Investments[1]

KEVIN G. CONWAY

*United Technologies Corporation*

The international tax rules in the Internal Revenue Code of 1986 ("the Code"), which are of major importance to companies such as United Technologies Corporation, were originally designed to level the playing field and ensure that U.S. corporations could compete on an equal footing with their international competitors based in other countries. The United States, unlike many other countries, has adopted a worldwide system of taxation. Under this system, U.S. corporations are subject to both foreign and federal income tax on profits earned outside the United States. This means that U.S. companies are liable for both U.S. tax and foreign tax on the same dollar of operating profit. This could result in U.S. corporations being taxed at a high level that would effectively render them noncompetitive. To alleviate this situation, the United States has adopted two major principles. First, under the principle of deferral a U.S. corporation is generally not subject to U.S. tax on profits earned by its subsidiaries located outside the United States until these profits are repatriated. The second major principle, the foreign tax credit, grants U.S. companies a credit against their U.S. tax when income earned outside the United States and previously subject to foreign income tax is repatriated to the United States. The credit is limited to the amount obtained by multiplying the U.S. tax times the fraction obtained by dividing foreign-source income by total taxable income. Besides leveling the playing field, this limitation is designed to avoid granting a foreign tax credit on U.S.-source income.

Recently, the term "corporate welfare" has been used to describe the international tax rules applicable to U.S.-based corporations. Use of the term corporate welfare is entirely inappropriate to describe the concepts of deferral and the foreign income tax credit. These rules do not grant any benefits but rather, as previ-

---

[1]The views and opinions expressed herein are solely those of the author.

ously noted, merely level the competitive playing field so that U.S.-based corporations can compete in the global marketplace.

With respect to the so-called 10-50 basket rule under the pre-1997 law and through a transition period, U.S.-based companies are at a competitive disadvantage in cases where they own more than a 10 percent interest, but not more than 50 percent ("a 10-50 joint venture"), of a non-U.S. enterprise. The disadvantage arises because under the 10-50 basket rule, a U.S. company that is a party to such a venture is required to prepare a separate foreign tax credit calculation for each 10-50 joint venture. In jurisdictions where the tax rate applicable to the 10-50 joint venture  is greater than the 35 percent U.S. corporate income tax rate, the U.S. shareholder will be unable to credit any taxes above the 35 percent rate against its U.S. income tax liability and thus will incur an increase in tax liability. For example, assume that a $100 dividend is paid from a country with a tax rate of 55 percent. The foreign taxes in excess of the U.S. tax liability would be $44 $((100/0.45) \times 35$ percent U.S. rate $- [(100/0.45) - 100)])$. On the other hand, where the non-U.S. rate is below the 35 percent U.S. rate, say, 20 percent, then any dividend repatriation from the 10-50 joint venture will result in a residual U.S. income tax (excess of 35 percent U.S. rate and 20 percent foreign rate, i.e., 15 percent) on the dividend distribution.

There are two effects of the 10-50 basket rule.  First is the paperwork associated with preparing a separate calculation for each so-called 10-50 joint venture.  Second, and more important, because the 10-50 basket rule may result in double taxation or the imposition of residual U.S. tax above the foreign taxes already paid, U.S. companies may not be competitive with their foreign counterparts.  As an illustration, I recall being involved in a negotiating regarding the acquisition of an interest in a company operating outside the United States. The owner would not sell a controlling interest but would sell 49 percent of the business.  The 10-50 rule applying to dividends paid by the joint venture thus altered the economics of the transaction. It needlessly complicates and is detrimental to our competitive position in an increasingly competitive global environment.  Congress finally recognized these issues and in the Taxpayer Relief Act of 1997 sought to correct them.  Effective for tax years beginning after December 31, 2002, a "look through" rule applied for these 10/50 companies. Thus, earnings may be accounted for in the appropriate basket after this date.  Dividends paid after the effective date of the Act by 10/50 companies but out of earnings before January 1, 2003 will be aggregated in a single 10/50 basket. This is a welcome step in improving our competitive position.

## GLOBAL COMPETITION FOR RESEARCH
## AND DEVELOPMENT INVESTMENTS

U.S. international companies are in a far different situation from that of several decades ago when substantially all the revenues, profits, and income tax expense of U.S.-based companies were sourced in the United States. In the case of United Technologies Corporation, more than 50 percent of our revenues and profits for 1996 and substantially more than 50 percent of our income tax expense are generated in jurisdictions outside the United States. We and other U.S.-based corporations are now paying significant income tax to foreign governments. This means that the research and development incentives and tax credits available outside the United States are more important than ever.

In these circumstances the United States needs to take a number of steps. First, we should stabilize the research incentives in the Code. The current research and experimentation (R&E) tax credit has been extended eight times, indicative of its popularity but also a source of great uncertainty as to whether or not the credit will even exist at the end of a taxable year. In view of the extended life and uncertain progress of research and development projects, it is clear that in order for the R&E tax incentive to be effective, companies must be able to rely on the existence of the credit beyond a single taxable year. In this regard, the 1996 Small Business Tax Act took a major step forward; it not only extended the credit but also modified it to take into account the changed economic circumstances of U.S.-based corporations. In this connection, the 1996 act introduced the alternative incremental research credit that is computed on a different base than the regular 20 percent incremental credit, which relies on a historical base period percentage derived from the years 1984-1988. The 1997 Taxpayer Relief Act extended both the regular and alternative incremental research credits. While this is encouraging, from a tax policy perspective, in order to be effective, the R&E credit must be viewed as a long-term and permanent incentive. In addition, the United States must periodically reexamine the mechanism of the credit, as it did recently with the alternative incremental credit, to make sure the credit is working properly as a tax incentive. Now to turn to incentives outside the United States.

At least 16 OECD (Organization for Economic Cooperation and Development) countries in addition to the United States offer significant research and development tax incentives and credits, some of them more generous than those offered in the United States. In addition, these are generally stable incentives that are maintained over an extended period of time and can be relied on by research personnel who typically have a horizon of five to ten years rather than just one tax year.

Canada has what I consider to be a very significant R&D tax incentive. Today, unlike previously, U.S. corporations that are paying significant taxes outside the United States have a choice of where they perform their R&D; if the choice is between the United States and Canada, Canada offers a major advantage. For example, consider a $100 R&D investment made in both jurisdictions. If that amount is invested in the United States the taxpayer receives a deduction equal to the U.S. income tax rate of 35 percent or $35.00. In addition, the U.S. company will receive an R&E tax credit if it meets the requirements for either the regular incremental credit or the new alternative incremental credit. Let us assume that the amount of the U.S. credit is equal to 10 percent. If we add the benefit of the tax deduction to the benefit of the tax credit we can see that the taxpayer has realized a benefit of $45.00 or 45 percent with respect to the $100.00 expenditure.

Now consider the tax treatment of the same $100.00 investment in R&D in the province of Quebec. Under the Canadian federal and provincial income tax rules a taxpayer investing $100.00 in R&D in Quebec would receive a combined federal and provincial credit of approximately 30 percent. In addition, the tax-payer would be entitled to a deduction at the combined federal and provincial rate of 40 percent on average, resulting in a total benefit of approximately 70 percent or $70. This compares to the $45 benefit in the case of the United States and constitutes a major competitive advantage. Given this choice and other consider-ations being equal, a U.S.-based corporation will choose to make the R&D in-vestment in Canada, reduce its tax burden and its effective tax rate, and maximize its profit. France, Japan, and other countries also have significant R&D tax de-ductions and tax credits. We need to take these incentives into account in evalu-ating our own system and considering changes in it.

## R&D INCENTIVES AND TAX REFORM

Last summer I testified before the House Ways and Means Committee re-garding the international tax rules, their current operation, and the potential im-pact of a flat tax or the USA (unlimited savings allowance) tax. At one point during the hearings, Representative Sam Gibbons of Florida asked the panel of which I was a member whether or not there would be a need for an R&E tax credit in the event a flat tax were passed. Representative Gibbons postulated that under a flat tax, a company would get a current deduction for all expenditures, there would be no allocations of R&D expenses against foreign-source income, and there would be no need for a tax credit. He asked the panel members if they concurred with this conclusion. I responded that there would still be a case for R&D tax incentives under a flat tax. I pointed to countries such as Australia and Malaysia that allow a deduction greater than 100 percent for R&D expenditures. This type of incentive would be compatible with a flat tax. Given the importance of R&D incentives to American industry and economic growth, I would favor a deduction of 150-200 percent for R&D in order to provide what I believe is the appropriate incentive.

Finally, we should remember the R&E tax credit is largely a wage credit. Recent studies by the Treasury Department and the Internal Revenue Service confirm that more than 60 cents of each dollar of research expense qualifying for the credit in fact represents salaries and wages paid to U.S. personnel (i.e., engi-neers, scientists, and others) who are located in the United States. We should not forget that the R&E tax credit promotes skilled jobs at home for U.S. citizens.

# III

## TAX REFORM: PRESCRIPTIONS AND PROSPECTS

# 8

# International Tax and Competitiveness Aspects of Fundamental Tax Reform[1]

PETER R. MERRILL
*Price Waterhouse LLP*

## INTRODUCTION

Continued growth of the U.S. economy into the twenty-first century is more dependent than ever on trade and investment ties with the world economy. Exports represent more than 11 percent of all the goods and services produced in the United States, and overseas investment accounts for more than 19 percent of corporate profits. In 1994, approximately 2,600 U.S. corporations operated more than 21,000 affiliates abroad.

As foreign economies have grown over the last three decades, their businesses have expanded overseas and now rival U.S. corporations in their international scope. Whereas 18 of the world's 100 largest companies were headquartered in the United States in the 1960s, only 8 of them are today. The United States is still the world's largest economy, but it now produces 25 percent of the world's output, compared to 40 percent in the 1960s.

The U.S. tax system and its interaction with foreign tax systems affects the cost of financing overseas investment and also the amount of such investment (Hubbard, 1995). Fundamental changes in U.S. tax policy have the potential to affect domestic as well as cross-border investment. Changes in U.S. tax policy also may have collateral effects on the U.S. tax treaty network depending on how foreign governments react. Thus, the international implications of fundamental tax reform cannot be ignored.

---

[1]The views expressed in this chapter are those of the author and should not be attributed to Price Waterhouse LLP.

## COMPARISON OF U.S. AND FOREIGN TAXATION OF
## INCOME FROM INTERNATIONAL OPERATIONS

A number of objectives have been advanced for the U.S. international income tax regime. In addition to the goal of raising sufficient tax revenues, these objectives include (U.S. Congress, 1992):

- *Efficient international capital allocation.* Taxes (other than taxes in the nature of user fees) should not distort firms' investment location decisions; in other words, private investment should flow to the locations that offer the highest pretax rates of return.
- *International tax competitiveness.* U.S.-owned investments should not be subject to higher taxes than foreign-owned investments in the same location.
- *Simplicity.* Compliance and administrative costs should be as low as possible.
- *Harmonization.* The United States should not depart unnecessarily from widely accepted international income tax norms.

As discussed below, the current U.S. income tax system does not fully achieve any of these objectives.

### Efficient International Capital Allocation

The efficiency objective can be achieved by taxing worldwide income on a uniform and current basis with an unlimited credit for foreign taxes (other than taxes in the nature of user fees).

The present U.S. tax system deviates from this efficient tax system in a number of respects. For example, (1) different depreciation rules apply to domestic and foreign investment; (2) losses of a foreign corporation cannot be consolidated with its U.S. parent; (3) the foreign tax credit is subject to numerous limitations; and (4) income earned through a foreign corporation generally is not taxed until repatriated.

Some have argued that the taxation of foreign direct investment may no longer be relevant for locational efficiency because international portfolio investment has become far more significant (Hufbauer, 1992; Frisch, 1992). Under this view, the marginal source of finance for international investment is international portfolio capital.

### International Tax Competitiveness

The competitiveness objective could be achieved by exempting foreign-source active business income from domestic taxation (i.e., territorial taxation), so that the only applicable income tax would be that imposed by the host country. The present U.S. income tax system differs from this internationally competitive tax system because the foreign investments of U.S. taxpayers can result in additional U.S. tax liability. This can occur because the taxpayer repatriates income from relatively low-tax foreign countries or because the foreign tax credit is limited artificially by the overallocation of U.S. expenses against foreign-source income.

Under one view of multinational investment, home-country taxes do not directly affect the investment decisions of "mature" subsidiaries that finance foreign investment from retained earnings (Hartman, 1985). Under this model, the imposition of U.S. tax on income earned in low-tax countries does not cause a competitiveness problem for mature foreign subsidiaries. A competitiveness issue arises, however, in the case of investments made out of parent equity rather than retained earnings of the foreign subsidiary.

Another view is that imposition of an "efficient" worldwide income tax system is consistent with international competitiveness because the burden of capital income taxation is borne fully by domestic savers. In this model the imposition of U.S. taxes on foreign investment does not put U.S. multinationals at a competitive disadvantage because U.S. investors are prepared to accept a lower net of tax return on this investment than investors who reside in countries that impose lower income taxes (Gravelle, 1996). With rising international capital mobility, however, one may question the assumption that a nation's capital income taxes are borne fully by resident savers.

## Harmonization

U.S. international tax rules frequently are more burdensome than those of other major industrialized countries such as France, Germany, and Japan (Granwell et al., 1996). As a result of these differences, the United States is generally considered an unattractive location, from the standpoint of corporate income taxes, for the establishment of corporate headquarters.

- The United States taxes the worldwide income of U.S. businesses and U.S. citizens. Many other countries exempt foreign-source business income either by statute (*e.g.*, France) or by treaty (*e.g.*, Germany).
- The U.S. foreign tax credit system requires complex calculations of separate limitations for different categories of income. The foreign tax credit systems of other countries generally are simpler.
- Virtually alone among the major industrial countries, the United States refuses to accept tax sparing provisions in its bilateral income tax treaties. Under a tax sparing agreement, the home country agrees to treat income that benefits from tax incentives in the host country as having been subject to tax at the normal rates. Developing countries often insist on tax sparing agreements as condition for entering into bilateral income tax treaties with capital exporting countries. Consequently, the U.S. treaty network is less extensive than that of most other major industrial countries.

- Most countries' anti-deferral regimes do not tax active business income but instead are limited to passive types of income. In contrast, the United States imposes current U.S. tax on several types of active business income as well as passive income.
- Unlike other major industrial countries, the United States treats a loan from a foreign subsidiary to its domestic parent as a deemed dividend, potentially triggering current U.S. tax on foreign income.
- The United States has more detailed and complex rules for allocating and apportioning expenses between domestic- and foreign-source income than does any other major industrialized country. These rules often conflict with source rules adopted by other countries, giving rise to the risk of double taxation.
- Unlike other countries, the United States imposes an alternative minimum tax that limits utilization of otherwise allowable foreign tax credits. This can result in U.S. tax being imposed on foreign income that has borne foreign income tax in excess of the U.S. rate.
- Unlike most other major industrial countries, the United States has a "classical" income tax system that imposes tax on corporate income at both the corporate and the shareholder levels.

## Simplification

The U.S. rules for taxing foreign-source income are among the most complicated in the world. The cost of complying with these rules represents a hidden tax on U.S.-based multinational companies. Recent research has confirmed that the international provisions of the U.S. tax code impose disproportionately high compliance burdens—both relative to U.S. tax rules for domestic income and relative to foreign countries' taxation of international income. For example, one survey of firms in the Internal Revenue Service's (IRS) large-case audit program found that nearly 40 percent of total federal income tax compliance costs are attributable to foreign-source income. This is disproportionately large compared to the average fraction of assets (21.1 percent), sales (24.1 percent), and employment (17.7 percent) abroad. By contrast, a survey of 965 European firms found no evidence that compliance costs were higher for foreign-source income than for domestic-source income (Blumenthal and Slemrod, 1994).

## Summary

The U.S. international tax system is a hybrid, with elements of residence- and source-based taxation. It does not adhere consistently to the principles of locational neutrality or international competitiveness; instead, present law may be viewed as a complex mixture of these principles. It is also fair to say that the effects of income tax rules on the behavior of multinational corporations are complex and not fully understood by economists. Consequently, the evaluation of international tax reform proposals depends, in part, on the model of multinational behavior that is assumed.

Since the changes in the international tax rules made by the 1986 Tax Reform Act, a number of bills have been introduced in Congress to make incremental reforms in the present international income tax rules.[2] In the 104th session of Congress, more fundamental tax reform proposals were introduced that would have replaced the income tax system with a consumption-based tax system. These fundamental tax reform proposals are discussed in the following section and in the last section of this chapter.

## FUNDAMENTAL TAX REFORM: KEY INTERNATIONAL ISSUES

Among the fundamental tax reform proposals introduced in the 104th Congress are S. 722, the Unlimited Savings Allowance (USA) Tax, sponsored by Senators Sam Nunn (D-GA) and Pete V. Domenici (R-NM); H.R. 2060, the Flat Tax, sponsored by House Majority Leader Dick Armey (R-TX); and H.R. 3039, the National Retail Sales Tax, sponsored by Representatives Dan Schaefer (R-CO) and Billy Tauzin (R-LA).

All of these proposals would eliminate the federal income tax and replace it with a new consumption-based tax system. Each of the three proposals would tax only U.S. operations. These bills would repeal most U.S. withholding taxes on income paid to foreign investors. U.S. businesses operating abroad would not be taxed on their foreign-source income, nor would dividends paid by foreign subsidiaries back to their U.S. parents be subject to U.S. tax. Because these systems generally exclude foreign operations from the U.S. tax base, they would eliminate the foreign tax credit rules and the complex rules taxing certain unrepatriated income of U.S.-controlled foreign corporations (subpart F of the tax code).

The fundamental tax reform proposals also raise certain new issues in the international context that have not yet been fully explored.

### Reactions of Other Countries

It is not clear how foreign governments would react to a decision by the United States to repeal its income tax system and replace it with a consumption-based tax. They might respond negatively by adopting new antiabuse rules or terminating existing tax treaties with the United States. Alternatively, they might opt to leave their treaties with the United States in place and perhaps lower their own taxes to retain U.S. investment.

---

[2]For example, the Rostenkowski-Gradison 1991 bill (H.R. 5270), the Houghton-Levin 1995 bill (H.R. 1690), and the Pressler-Baucus 1996 bill (S. 2086). Some of the provisions contained in these bills were enacted in the Taxpayer Relief Act of 1997.

One of the features of the U.S. consumption tax proposals that may concern our trading partners is their proposed elimination of taxes on virtually all investment, including income from the portfolio investments of foreign residents. Indeed, eliminating the income tax system and replacing it with a system that exempts portfolio income could well turn the United States into a tax haven from the perspective of other countries (Avi-Yonah, 1995).

Although the consumption tax proposals would alleviate U.S. concerns regarding transfer pricing practices and earnings stripping, they likely would exacerbate foreign concerns about these same issues (Grubert and Newlon, 1995; Avi-Yonah, 1996)

In response to these concerns, foreign governments might either pursue an approach similar to that of the United States—that is, lower their taxes on investment as well—or attempt to capture the revenue forgone by the United States. This latter option could involve taxing their resident multinationals on worldwide profits, including U.S.-source profits.[3] In addition, foreign governments could impose new antiabuse rules; for example, they might enact earnings stripping rules that limit the deduction of interest paid to U.S. affiliates. Foreign governments might also deny a foreign tax credit for U.S. taxes. Foreign governments also might consider nontax measures, including capital controls, to stem the potential flow of capital into the United States.

### Risks to the U.S. Tax Treaty Network

If the United States adopted one of the leading consumption-based tax reform proposals, it is not clear how the U.S. tax treaty network would be affected. The United States now has bilateral income tax treaties with nearly 50 countries. The treaties provide numerous benefits to investors, including reduced withholding tax rates on income flows between the United States and the treaty partner.

Under the USA Tax, the Flat Tax, and the National Retail Sales Tax, U.S. withholding taxes on the income of foreign corporate investors generally would be repealed. Therefore, the reduced withholding tax rates under the treaties no longer would confer a special benefit to foreign treaty partners. As a result, U.S. tax treaty partners—all of whom have some form of income tax system—may view themselves as providing benefits to U.S. investors while their own investors receive few benefits from the United States under these income tax treaties. Accordingly, treaty partners may believe they have little to gain by continuing their existing tax treaty relationships with the United States, or by reducing cross-border withholding tax rates in future treaty negotiations.

On the other hand, many treaty partners may wish to maintain their treaties with the United States to preserve certain other benefits provided under the agreements. In addition to lowering withholding rates, tax treaties also include guid-

---

[3]See Avi-Yonah (1996, p. 262).

ance on a number of important issues, such as rules for determining each country's jurisdiction to tax multinational business income, as well as on numerous industry-specific questions. In addition, treaty partners might decide to maintain a treaty relationship with the United States because imposing the higher statutory withholding rates on U.S. investors would make foreign jurisdictions less attractive as locations for U.S. investment.

### Trade, Transfer Pricing, and the "Origin" and "Destination" Principles

The leading tax restructuring proposals differ in their treatment of exports and imports. Both the National Retail Sales Tax proposal and the USA Business Tax are "destination-based" taxes. Under the destination principle, imports are taxed and exports are exempt, and the tax base generally would be consumption of goods and services within the United States. By contrast, the Flat Tax is an "origin-based" tax. Under the origin principle, exports are taxed and imports are not. Under the Flat Tax, the tax base generally would be consumption plus net exports.[4]

Some observers believe that destination-based taxes promote exports and discourage imports. Despite the intuitive appeal of this idea, economists generally believe that destination-based taxes offer no long-term export incentives (Grubert and Newlon, 1995, p. 628. See also Grossman, 1980; Dixit, 1985; and Feldstein and Krugman, 1990.) In any event, destination-based taxes do offer other advantages over origin-based taxes. Foremost among these advantages is greater administrability—particularly in the area of transfer pricing.

Under a destination-based tax, transfer prices generally would *not* be relevant to determining U.S. tax liability. Because export sales—and presumably also royalty receipts from abroad—would be exempt, and imports—including royalty payments to foreign parties—would be nondeductible, the prices set for such transactions would not affect the U.S. tax base. Accordingly, there would be little opportunity to use transfer prices to reduce U.S. taxes. Rather, multinationals would have an incentive to shift profits out of other countries that impose income taxes and into the United States (by inflating interest and royalty payments to the United States); (Avi-Yonah, 1995, p. 917); (Grubert and Newlon, 1995, p. 637).

By contrast, under an origin-based tax, such as the Flat Tax, transfer pricing would continue to be a concern from a U.S. perspective because export sales would be taxable and imports would be deductible.

It is important to note that all of the major consumption-based tax alternatives would eliminate certain export incentives provided under our current income tax system. Repeal of current foreign sales corporation and export source

---

[4]Disregarding the individual standard deduction and personal exemption that reduce the potential tax base.

rules could shift the composition of exports away from manufacturing and toward services.[5]

## Legality Under International Trade Rules

Another issue is whether a move to a consumption-based tax system with "border tax adjustments" would pass muster under international trade rules. This question already has been raised with respect to at least one fundamental tax reform proposal—the USA Business Tax. International trade rules generally permit border adjustments for indirect taxes, such as value-added taxes, but they bar these adjustments under direct taxes, such as income taxes.

Although the USA Business Tax is similar to a value-added tax, it is drafted as a direct tax and therefore might be challenged under trade rules. Another feature of the USA Tax that might cause concerns is the credit it provides for payroll taxes—a feature not present in foreign value-added tax (VAT) systems. It is possible that a payroll tax credit could be viewed as inconsistent with GATT requirements (Summers, 1996).

## Foreign Direct Investment

By itself, adoption of a consumption tax would have little effect on the location of investment because imposition of a consumption tax does not alter the rate of return on the marginal investment (whether in the United States or abroad). Repeal of the U.S. income tax system, however, would likely have important effects on the magnitude and composition of both inbound and outbound foreign direct investment.

Absent reaction by foreign governments, inbound investment would be attracted to the United States, particularly from countries with territorial tax systems. Unless U.S. interest rates fall substantially, the elimination of interest deductibility would cause equity financing to become relatively more attractive compared to debt financing for foreign investors in the United States.

In the case of outbound investment, U.S. investors would likely shift investment away from high-tax foreign jurisdictions and into the United States and low-tax foreign jurisdictions. Absent a decline in U.S. interest rates, U.S. multinationals would be expected to reduce debt financing in the United States and to increase debt abroad.

## R&D AND TECHNOLOGY ISSUES

The leading proposals to restructure the U.S. tax system could have a significant impact on decisions relating to the development and use of technology. All three leading tax reform proposals—the USA Tax, the Flat Tax, and the National Retail

---

[5]The Taxpayer Relief Act of 1997 extended the tax benefit of foreign sales corporations to software exports.

Sales Tax—would represent a major break from the current-law treatment of R&D. None of the three proposals would retain the research and experimentation (R&E) tax credit and none would provide any incentive for performing R&D activities.

As discussed below, these and other effects of the various proposals on R&D expenditures should be weighed carefully to ensure that one of the main goals of tax restructuring advocates—increasing the national rate of economic growth—is not undermined by inadvertently causing a decline in R&D spending in the United States (National Commission on Economic Growth and Tax Reform, 1996[6]).

## Tax Treatment of R&D Under Present Law

Since 1981, the U.S. income tax has provided an explicit incentive to boost the level of R&D above the level that otherwise would occur in the marketplace. The regular R&E tax credit under section 41 provides a 20 percent credit for the amount by which a taxpayer's qualified research expenditures—generally comprised of wages and supplies—for a taxable year exceed a base amount.[7] The base amount generally is calculated as the product of the taxpayer's "fixed base percentage" and the average annual gross receipts of the taxpayer for the four preceding taxable years. The "fixed base percentage" generally is equal to the percentage that aggregate qualified research expenditures for the five fiscal years 1984-1988 is of aggregate gross receipts over the period.

In 1996, Congress added an alternative incremental tax credit (AIRC) with rates of 1.65, 2.20, and 2.75 percent for research in excess of 1.0, 1.5, and 2.0 percent, respectively, of average annual gross receipts during the four preceding years. Once the AIRC is elected, it can be revoked only with the consent of the Secretary of the Treasury. The purpose of the AIRC is to provide an incremental incentive for companies to increase research expenditures in situations where changes in business conditions since the 1984-1988 base period have caused the fixed base percentage to become out of date.

A tax system's impact on R&D is not limited to its treatment of costs relating to the *development* of new technologies. The tax treatment of the *utilization* of these technologies also plays a role in taxpayer decisions relating to R&D activities. For many high-technology companies, a key issue is how U.S. international tax rules treat income derived from exploiting the use of an intangible asset overseas.

Royalties received for the use of intangible assets outside the United States generally are considered territorially to be foreign-source income for purposes of the foreign tax credit. Under the so-called look-through rules, foreign royalties

---

[6]According to the report of the National Commission on Economic Growth and Tax Reform, "attention must be given to the proper tax treatment of foreign-source license fees, royalties, and other intangibles so as not to discourage research and development in the United States."

[7]Deductions allowed under section 174 are reduced by an amount equal to 100 percent of the taxpayer research credit. In lieu of reducing section 174 deductions, taxpayers may elect to claim a reduced credit.

generally are treated as "active" income with the result that low-tax foreign royalties and high-tax foreign dividends may be averaged for purposes of determining the foreign tax credit limitation. This allows increased utilization of foreign tax credits.

Withholding taxes often are imposed by foreign governments on the gross amount of royalty payments. The current U.S. income tax treaty network generally serves to reduce withholding taxes on royalties to the extent possible. Withholding taxes generally are creditable for U.S. tax purposes.

Also of importance for many high-technology companies are the current-law rules requiring apportionment of domestic research expenses between U.S. and foreign-source income. Domestic research expenses that are apportioned to foreign-source income reduce the foreign tax credit limitations. As a result, for every $100 of domestic research allocated to foreign-source income, foreign tax credits may be reduced by as much as $35 at the current 35 percent U.S. corporate tax rate. This loss in foreign tax credit is tantamount to treating the foreign-allocated portion of U.S. research expenses as nondeductible.

## Tax Restructuring Proposals

Leading proposals to restructure the U.S. tax system could affect decisions relating to the development and utilization of technology. The USA Tax and the Flat Tax have in common the replacement of the federal corporate income tax with a new business tax. These new business taxes in many respects would make a radical break with current law:

- *No R&E credit*: Neither the USA Tax nor the Flat Tax would retain the R&E tax credit. There is no explicit incentive for performing R&D activities in either bill. In drafting their USA Tax proposal, Senators Nunn and Domenici initially explored the question whether their proposed business tax could accommodate an R&E tax credit or some other type of incentive for research activities.[8] It is unclear why the drafters of the USA Tax decided not to include a research credit in their bill. It is possible that the drafters were concerned that inclusion of a research credit could jeopardize the legality of border tax adjustments under the GATT. Unlike the USA Tax, however, the Armey Flat Tax does not have border adjustments; consequently, GATT considerations would not preclude inclusion of a research tax credit in a Flat Tax system.
- *Expensing for certain costs now capitalized*: Some aspects of tax restructuring proposals as they relate to R&D activities would be more favorable than current law. Both the USA Tax and the Flat Tax would allow current

---

[8]In a letter (Oct. 21, 1994) to then-Treasury Secretary Lloyd Bentsen, Senators Nunn and Domenici asked, "Would a business cash-flow tax as described which also includes an R&E tax credit similar to current code Section 41's research and development credit for wages paid for qualified research services qualify for border adjustment under GATT?"

deductions for all business purchases. Thus, for example, amounts paid for laboratory facilities, equipment, and certain intangible assets in conjunction with R&D activities could be deducted currently rather than depreciated or amortized over a period of years. However, R&D activities appear to be relatively labor intensive compared to other business activities. A reduction in the tax burden on capital income, which would occur under fundamental tax reform, would shift investment away from labor-intensive sectors.

- *Treatment of royalties*: The USA Tax would not tax exports of goods and services. Foreign-source royalty income would be treated as an export for this purpose. Thus, a U.S. company that licensed a technology for use overseas would not include royalty income from the licensing arrangement in its taxable gross receipts. The Flat Tax would appear to provide less favorable treatment for foreign-source royalty income. Although the statutory language of the Armey bill does not specifically address the treatment of royalties and license fees received from abroad, it is clear that export income as a general rule would be subject to tax. Foreign withholding taxes levied on royalties and other income would not be deductible or creditable under the Flat Tax.
- *Impact on withholding taxes*: As discussed above, it is possible that existing treaties—and withholding rates—might be jeopardized if the United States unilaterally were to eliminate its income tax system. This raises the possibility of a significant increase in foreign withholding taxes levied on the return to U.S. technology licensed abroad.
- *No allocation of R&D expenses*: Both the USA Tax and the Flat Tax are territorial taxes. Under these systems, there would be no foreign tax credit and no allocation of R&D expenses between U.S. and foreign sources.
- *Treatment of compensation-related expenses:* Compensation-related expenses are not deductible under the USA Business Tax, whereas wages and salaries (but not fringe benefits and payroll taxes) are deductible under the Flat Tax.

## Static Effects of USA Business Tax and the Flat Tax on R&D

The potential effects of the USA and Flat Taxes can be illustrated by means of a simple example *(see Appendix)*. The example posits a U.S. multinational that spends $100 million on research in the United States, of which $42 million represents qualified research expenses for purposes of the research credit.[9] Of the

---

[9]R&D reported on Securities and Exchange Commission Form 10-K by public corporations included in the COMPUSTAT database amounted to $102 billion for fiscal years ending in 1992. The IRS reports corporate taxpayers claimed $43.3 billion of qualified research expense (QRE) for tax years ending July 1, 1992, through June 30, 1993. The ratio of QRE to R&D, therefore, is estimated as 42 percent.

$100 million in total research expenses, $52 million is wages and salaries; $6.24 million, employee benefits; $3.98 million, payroll tax; $15 million, depreciation; and $22.78 million, other expenses (U.S. Congress, 1995).[10]

In 1994, the research tax credit amounted to 4.4 percent of qualified research expenses, so the hypothetical taxpayer in this example is assumed to be able to claim a research credit of $1.85 million (4.4 percent of $42 million of qualified research expense).[11]

The taxpayer's R&D activities result in patents and other valuable intangible assets that produce U.S. income and foreign income. For purposes of this example, it is assumed that half of the income from the intangible assets is earned in the United States and the other half is attributable to foreign royalties. The taxpayer's foreign royalties are subject to an average withholding tax rate of 5 percent.[12] U.S. multinationals are required to allocate domestic research expense between U.S. and foreign sources for purposes of computing the foreign tax credit. In this example, the taxpayer allocates 25 percent of U.S. research expense to foreign sources.[13] For simplicity, the example includes only items of income and expense directly related to R&D, and the taxpayer is assumed not to be subject to the alternative minimum tax.

Under present law, if the expired R&E tax credit were extended, the hypothetical taxpayer would have to earn $90.7 million to break even on $100 million of R&D if the taxpayer was in an excess foreign tax credit position and $98.2 million if in a deficit foreign tax credit position. The break-even return is less than the $100 million cost of R&D due to the research credit ($1.85 million) and, in the case of the excess foreign tax credit taxpayer, the utilization of foreign tax credits (in excess of the 5 percent withholding tax on the royalty).

The impact of the USA Business Tax and the Flat Tax on the cost of performing R&D in the United States can be measured by calculating the change in return required to break even on $100 million of R&D for the taxpayer in the preceding example. The 11 percent USA Tax is intended to be revenue neutral. By contrast, the 17 percent Flat Tax introduced by Representative Armey would raise less revenue than current law. For the sake of comparability, the Flat Tax also is analyzed at a 21 percent rate, which has been determined by the Treasury

---

[10]The Office of Technology Assessment estimates that 62 percent of research expense is allocable to compensation. The employer's share of payroll taxes is calculated at the statutory 7.65 percent rate, and employee benefits (excluding payroll taxes) are assumed to be 12 percent of wages.

[11]Data provided by the IRS Statistics of Income Division based on Forms 6765 filed for tax years ending July 1, 1993, through June 30, 1994.

[12]The United States seeks to obtain a zero withholding tax rate on royalties in its bilateral income tax treaties, but many treaties provide for a 5 percent or higher rate such as the U.S. treaties with Australia, Canada, China, France, India, Italy, Japan, and Spain. (See Price Waterhouse LLP, 1996.)

[13]Under regulations, taxpayers that use the gross sales method generally may allocate 50 percent of U.S. research expense to U.S. source income and then apportion the remaining 50 percent on the basis of U.S. and foreign sales.

**TABLE 8.1** Percentage Increase in Break-even Rate of Return on Domestic R&D Over Present Law—Static Effects

| Tax Regime | Taxpayer With Excess Foreign Tax Credits (%) | Taxpayer Without Excess Foreign Tax Credits (%) |
|---|---|---|
| USA Tax | 09.9 | 1.5 |
| Armey Flat Tax (17%) | 15.6 | 6.8 |
| Revenue-neutral Flat Tax (21%) | 16.4 | 7.6 |

SOURCE: Price Waterhouse LLP calculations (see Appendix).

Department as necessary to achieve revenue neutrality (U.S. Department of the Treasury, 1996).

Under the USA Business Tax, the break-even return on $100 million of R&D would be $99.6 million under the facts of the example. Thus, for the taxpayer in this example, the USA Tax would increase the after-tax cost of R&D by about 2-10 percent, depending on whether or not the taxpayer currently is in an excess foreign tax credit position. The potential rise in the after-tax cost of R&D primarily is attributable to the loss of the research and foreign tax credits and the inability to deduct compensation and payroll taxes.

As shown in Table 8.1, under the Armey Flat Tax, the break-even return on $100 million of R&D would be $104.9 million at a 17 percent rate and $105.6 million at a 21 percent rate. Thus, for the taxpayer in this example, the 21-percent Flat Tax would increase the after-tax cost of R&D by about 8-16 percent compared to present law, depending on whether or not the taxpayer is in an excess foreign tax credit position. The rise in the after-tax cost of R&D primarily is attributable to the loss of the R&E credit, the taxation of foreign royalties with no credit or deduction for foreign withholding taxes, and the inability to deduct payroll taxes and employee benefits.

## Dynamic Effects

Under conventional incidence assumptions, taxes imposed on compensation costs are ultimately borne by workers. In addition, it commonly is assumed that a single-rate broad-based sales tax or value-added tax will cause a corresponding increase in the price level, as a result of accommodating monetary policy.

*Example*

Under the above assumption, the break-even return on $100 million of R&D under the USA Business Tax or the Flat Tax is $100 million plus foreign withholding taxes grossed up by the applicable marginal tax rate. Consequently, the break-even return on $100 million of R&D would be $102.6 million under the

**TABLE 8.2**   Percent Increase in Break-Even Rate of Return on Domestic
R&D over Present Law—Dynamic Effects

| Tax Regime | Taxpayer With Excess Foreign Tax Credits (%) | Taxpayer Without Excess Foreign Tax Credits (%) |
|---|---|---|
| USA Tax | 13.1 | 4.5 |
| Armey Flat Tax (17%) | 13.7 | 5.0 |
| Revenue-neutral Flat Tax (21%) | 13.9 | 5.2 |

NOTE: Business taxes imposed on compensation costs are assumed to be borne by workers; USA
Business Tax is fully passed forward in prices.

SOURCE: Price Waterhouse LLP calculations (see Appendix).

USA Business Tax, $103.1 million under the 17 percent Flat Tax, and $103.3
million under the 21 percent Flat Tax. This represents about a 5-14 percent increase in the after-tax cost of R&D, compared to present law, under both the Flat
Tax and the USA Business Tax (see Table 8.2).

## INCREMENTAL REFORM OF THE INCOME TAX SYSTEM

As an alternative to fundamental tax reform, incremental changes to the existing income tax system could be adopted. Reforms to the current system could
help address numerous areas of complexity in the international provisions of the
tax code.

### Foreign Tax Credit

The United States taxes its citizens, residents, and domestic corporations on
a worldwide basis and seeks to alleviate international double taxation through the
foreign tax credit. The foreign tax credit, however, is subject to significant limitations. Although foreign rules determine the amount of foreign tax imposed
(subject to U.S. currency translation rules), foreign-source income must be rede-
termined under U.S. rules for purposes of the foreign tax credit. The differences
between the U.S. and foreign definitions of taxable income—particularly the rules
on the sourcing of income and the allocation of deductions—create complexity
and increase the risk of double taxation. Other countries with foreign tax credit
systems frequently seek to promote harmony, minimize complexity, and avoid
double taxation by using the foreign jurisdiction's definition of taxable income
for foreign tax credit proposes.

Of particular note is the method by which U.S. interest expense is allocated
between domestic and foreign sources. Under present law, U.S. interest expense
is allocated between domestic- and foreign-source income according to a mea-

sure of domestic and foreign assets. Foreign interest expense, however, is allocated entirely to foreign-source income. The use of a "water's-edge" fungibility principle, rather than a "global" fungibility principle, to allocate interest expense systematically understates foreign-source income and overstates domestic-source income for purposes of the foreign tax credit.

In addition, U.S. rules impose numerous limitations on the availability of foreign tax credits, which bring their own complexities and further erode the effectiveness of the foreign tax credit mechanism in reducing double taxation. For example, separate limitations apply to eight special categories (or "baskets") of income. In addition, U.S. taxpayers that own interests of between 10 and 50 percent in foreign companies must compute a separate foreign tax credit limitation for each such company.[14] Moreover, these separate limitations impose substantial administrative complexity on U.S. firms attempting to calculate the amount of foreign tax credit to which they are entitled. Measures to simplify and streamline the foreign tax credit rules could greatly reduce the compliance burdens faced by U.S. businesses competing abroad.

It has become increasingly clear that the foreign tax credit system, since it was modified in 1986, imposes unacceptable compliance and enforcement burdens on taxpayers and tax authorities alike. Large companies must devote substantial resources each year to obtain and process from sources all over the world the information that is needed for the foreign tax credit computation. It has become impossible for U.S. multinationals to perform the actual computations without the aid of sophisticated computer software, and it is impossible for the IRS to audit these computations without relying on such software. These tasks certainly would be simplified by proposals to reduce the number of foreign tax credit baskets required by current law. Thus it is time to consider replacing the basket approach entirely with some simpler foreign tax credit system or even with a territorial income tax system (described below).

## Anti-deferral Rules

The United States generally does not tax U.S. shareholders on foreign-source income earned through a foreign corporation until such income is repatriated to the United States, just as it does not tax individual U.S. taxpayers on the earnings of corporations in which they own stock until dividends are declared and paid. This deferral is intended to permit U.S. taxpayers to compete internationally by reinvesting their foreign earnings without subjecting such earnings to current U.S. income taxation.

The United States, however, has adopted significant anti-deferral regimes that generally tax U.S. shareholders currently on certain types of undistributed

---

[14]The Taxpayer Relief Act of 1997 eliminates the separate foreign tax credit calculation for taxable years beginning after 2002.

foreign income as if such income were repatriated. Although other developed countries also limit the extent to which their taxpayers may defer tax on certain income earned by affiliated foreign corporations, U.S. rules are considerably more far-reaching and complex.

For example, the anti-deferral regimes of other developed countries generally eliminate deferral only for passive income. In contrast, U.S. anti-deferral regimes also eliminate deferral for many types of *active* trade or business income, including financial services income, international shipping and aircraft income, and certain other types of income.

Unlike other developed countries, which generally have only one anti-deferral regime, the United States has six. These regimes, enacted piecemeal over the last half-century, reflect a series of responses to perceived shortcomings in the deferral rules existing at the time of enactment. The aggregate result is a "patchwork" system that requires current taxation of certain types of income by reference to different factors and criteria (or imposes an interest charge on certain actual or deemed dispositions). The multiplicity and complexity of these anti-deferral regimes impose significant compliance costs on U.S. taxpayers and represent heavy administrative burdens for U.S. tax administrators.

Policymakers should give serious thought to consolidating the existing regimes and modifying their scope to achieve greater consistency with the anti-deferral rules imposed by our major trading partners.[15] Many other countries apply a much simpler effective foreign tax rate test or impose current tax only on active business income from specified low-tax countries. Such alternatives may not ultimately prove preferable to the basic U.S. approach, but they should be given serious consideration in any fundamental reform process (U.S. Department of the Treasury, 1993).

## Alternative Minimum Tax

The stated purpose of the alternative minimum tax (AMT) is "to ensure that no taxpayer with substantial economic income can avoid significant tax liability by using exclusions, deductions and credits."[16] This purpose is accomplished by imposing an AMT to the extent that AMT liability exceeds regular tax liability.

Under regular income tax rules, a U.S. taxpayer may claim a foreign tax credit for foreign taxes paid up to 100 percent of its U.S. tax liability on foreign source income. This system seeks to prevent double taxation of foreign source income. For taxpayers subject to the AMT, however, the foreign tax credit may offset no more than 90 percent of a taxpayer's AMT liability. Not only does this limitation on the foreign tax credit lack any clear economic rationale, it also appears inconsistent with certain U.S. treaty obligations.

---

[15]The Taxpayer Relief Act of 1997 provides that U.S.-controlled foreign corporations will not be subject to the passive foreign investment company (PFIC) rules after 1997.

[16]S. Rep. No. 99-313, 99th Congress, 2d Sess. 518-519 (1986).

## TERRITORIAL INCOME TAXATION

Another option would be to retain an income tax system but move from worldwide taxation to a territorial tax system for taxing foreign income. A "territorial" or "exemption" tax system is used in some form, either by statute or by treaty, by more than a dozen major industrialized countries, including the Netherlands, France, Germany, and Canada. Rather than merely deferring tax until foreign-source income is repatriated, countries with territorial income tax systems exempt the active business income earned abroad by their multinationals. Multinationals based in such countries, therefore, pay only the local tax imposed in countries in which they do business.

A move to a territorial income tax system could promote the competitiveness of U.S. multinationals by exempting foreign-source dividends and branch income. This could help ensure that foreign subsidiaries do not pay more tax in the aggregate on corporate income than do their foreign-based competitors in foreign markets. It is not clear, however, that a move to a territorial income tax system would greatly simplify current law for all taxpayers. Because passive investment income presumably would be taxed currently, look-through, anti-deferral, and foreign tax credit rules generally would remain necessary for passive foreign income. Transfer pricing issues would be at least as important under a territorial income tax system as they are today. Finally, it is important to note that a territorial income tax could actually increase U.S. tax on foreign-source royalties and export income compared to current U.S. law. Under a territorial system, excess foreign tax credits on high-tax dividends no longer would be available to reduce U.S. tax on foreign-source royalties and export income.[17]

## CONCLUSION

Although the international tax impact of various fundamental tax reform proposals thus far has not received the same attention as the domestic aspects of these proposals, they could have profound effects on the ability of U.S. companies and U.S. workers to compete in the global marketplace. Lawmakers must be careful to give full consideration to these international issues as they weigh replacement tax alternatives.

A switch to a consumption-based tax system could provoke undesirable reactions from our trading partners. A unilateral move to a consumption tax system could prompt trading partners to impose antiabuse rules and other measures aimed at capturing the taxes forgone by the United States. Our trading partners may feel compelled to take these steps to prevent taxpayers from shifting profits into the United States and, thereby, eroding their tax bases. In addition, our tax treaty

---

[17]The President's fiscal year 1998 Budget proposes to repeal the current export sales source rule and replace it with an "activities-based" method of sourcing income from the export of inventory property.

partners may consider terminating tax treaties because these agreements no longer would confer significant benefits from the United States. This could result in serious hardships for U.S. firms, which in the absence of the treaties would become subject to higher foreign withholding tax rates. Both of these possibilities—the expansion of foreign taxing jurisdiction and the abrogation of tax treaties—should cause policymakers to think carefully before undertaking any radical overhaul of the current tax system. In addition, each of the leading fundamental tax reform proposals could increase tax burdens on U.S. technology and U.S. exports, with potentially harmful effects on the economy.

Incremental reforms also may offer a possible alternative to the various fundamental tax reform proposals. Such incremental reforms could go a long way toward addressing provisions of U.S. tax law that are overly complex or discriminate against investment abroad.

A territorial income tax system is another alternative worthy of serious consideration if a consumption-based tax system is not adopted. However, it is not yet clear whether a move to such a system would be an improvement. Although a territorial income tax system would, in theory, help multinational businesses, it may not be a panacea. In practice, this approach could result in stiffer taxes on foreign-source royalties and exports without eliminating the need for transfer pricing rules or an anti-deferral regime for passive income.

## REFERENCES

Avi-Yonah, R.S. 1995. "The international implications of tax reform." *Tax Notes* (November):913, 922.

Avi-Yonah, R.S. 1996. "Comment on Grubert and Newlon." *National Tax Journal* 49(2):259, 262.

Blumenthal, M., and J.B. Slemrod. 1994. "The compliance cost of taxing foreign-source income: Its magnitude, determinants, and policy implications." In *National Tax Policy in an International Economy: Summary of Conference Papers*. Washington, D.C.: International Tax Policy Forum.

Dixit, A. 1985. "Tax policy in open economies." In *Handbook of Public Economics*, A. Auerbach and M. Feldstein, eds. Amsterdam: North-Holland.

Feldstein, M., and P. Krugman. 1990. "International effects of value-added taxation." Pp. 263-278 in *Taxation in the Global Economy*, A. Razin and J. Slemrod, eds. Chicago: University of Chicago Press.

Frisch, D. 1992. "The economics of international tax policy: Some old and new approaches." *Tax Notes* (April):581-591.

Granwell, A., P. Merrill, and C. Dubert. 1996. *Taxation of U.S. Corporations Doing Business Abroad: U.S. Rules and Competitiveness Issues*, Chapter 9. Morristown, New Jersey: Financial Executives Research Foundation.

Gravelle, J.G. 1996. *Foreign Tax Provisions of the American Jobs Act of 1996*. Washington, D.C.: Congressional Research Service.

Grossman, G.M. 1980. "Border tax adjustments: Do they distort trade?" *Journal of International Economics 10* (February):117-128.

Grubert, H., and T.S. Newlon. 1995. "The international implications of consumption tax proposals." *National Tax Journal* 48(4):619.

Hartman, D. 1985. "Tax policy and foreign direct investment." *Journal of Public Economics* 26(1):107-121.

Hubbard, R.G. 1995. "U.S. tax policy and foreign direct investment: Incentives, problems, and reforms." *Tax Policy and Economic Growth*. Washington, D.C.: American Council for Capital Formation.

Hufbauer, G. 1992. *U.S.Taxation of International Income: Blueprint for Reform*. Washington, D.C.: Institute for International Economics.

National Commission on Economic Growth and Tax Reform. 1996. *Unleashing America's Potential: A Pro-Growth, Pro-Family Tax System for the 21st Century*. Washington, D.C.: National Commission on Economic Growth and Tax Reform.

Price Waterhouse LLP. 1996. Corporate Taxes: A Worldwide Survey (1996 Edition). New York, New York.

Summers, V. 1996. "The border adjustability of consumption taxes, existing and proposed." *Tax Notes International* 1793, 1800.

U.S. Congress, House of Representatives. 1992. Statement of Fred T. Goldberg, Jr., Assistant Secretary (Tax Policy), U.S. Department of the Treasury, before the Committee on Ways and Means. Serial no. 102-176.

U.S. Congress, Office of Technology Assessment. 1995. Pp. 19-20 in *The Effectiveness of Research and Experimentation Tax Credits*. Washington, D.C.: U.S. Government Printing Office.

U.S. Department of the Treasury. 1993. *International Tax Reform: An Interim Report*. Washington, D.C.

U.S. Department of the Treasury. 1996. "New Armey-Shelby flat tax would still lose money, Treasury finds." Office of Tax Analysis. Reprinted in *Tax Notes* (January):451-61.

# APPENDIX

## Static Effect of Tax Restructuring Proposals on the Tax Treatment of R&D: Example

ASSUMPTIONS

| | | | |
|---|---|---|---|
| Foreign share of return | 50 percent | | |
| Foreign withholding tax | 5 percent | | |

| | Total | Qualified | Nonqualified |
|---|---|---|---|
| R&D expenses (section. 174) | 100.00 | 42.00 | 58.00 |
| Wages and salaries | 52.00 | 22.00 | 30.00 |
| Employer share of payroll tax | 3.98 | NA | 3.98 |
| Employee benefits | 6.24 | NA | 6.24 |
| Fixed cost (depreciation) | 15.00 | NA | 15.00 |
| Other | 22.78 | 20.00 | 2.78 |
| U.S. R&D allocated to U.S. source | 75% | | |

| | Present Law | | Flat Tax | | USA Tax |
|---|---|---|---|---|---|
| Item | Excess FTC | Deficit FTC | Armey-Shelby | Revenue neutral | Nunn-Domenici |
| Tax status | | | | | |
| Tax rate | 35% | 35% | 17% | 21% | 11% |
| Effective rate of R&D credit | 4.4% | 4.4% | NA | NA | NA |
| Foreign tax credit position | Excess | Deficit | NA | NA | NA |
| AMT | no | no | NA | NA | NA |
| Gross income | 90.68 | 98.15 | 104.87 | 105.56 | 99.63 |
| U.S. source | 45.34 | 49.08 | 52.44 | 52.78 | 49.82 |
| Foreign royalty, gross of withholding tax | 45.34 | 49.08 | 52.44 | 52.78 | 49.82 |
| Withholding tax | 2.27 | 2.45 | 2.62 | 2.64 | 2.49 |
| Research expense (section 174) | 100.00 | 100.00 | 100.00 | 100.00 | 100.00 |
| U.S. source | 75.00 | 75.00 | 100.00 | 100.00 | 100.00 |
| Foreign source | 25.00 | 25.00 | 0.00 | 0.00 | 0.00 |
| Components of research expense | | | | | |
| Wages | 52.00 | 52.00 | 52.00 | 52.00 | 52.00 |
| Payroll tax | 3.98 | 3.98 | 3.98 | 3.98 | 3.98 |
| Benefits | 6.24 | 6.24 | 6.24 | 6.24 | 6.24 |
| Capital cost recovery[a] | 15.00 | 15.00 | 16.86 | 16.86 | 16.86 |
| Other[b] | 22.78 | 22.78 | 22.78 | 22.78 | 22.78 |
| Qualified research expense | 42.00 | 42.00 | NA | NA | NA |
| Taxable income | −7.47 | 0.00 | 13.23 | 13.92 | 10.17 |
| U.S. tax before credits | −2.62 | 0.00 | 2.25 | 2.92 | 1.12 |
| Credits | 8.97 | 4.30 | 0.00 | 0.00 | 3.98 |
| Research credit | 1.85 | 1.85 | NA | NA | NA |
| Foreign tax credit | 7.12 | 2.45 | NA | NA | NA |
| Payroll tax credit | NA | NA | NA | NA | 3.98 |
| U.S. tax after credits | −11.58 | −4.30 | 2.25 | 2.92 | −2.86 |
| U.S. and foreign tax | −9.32 | −1.85 | 4.87 | 5.56 | −0.37 |
| Research expense after U.S. and foreign tax | 90.68 | 98.15 | 104.87 | 105.56 | 99.63 |

NOTE: FTC = foreign tax credit

[a]R&D capital costs generally are five-year property under present law but would be expenses under a consumption tax. With 7% annual growth, steady-state ratio of depreciation to investment is 89%.

[b]Amount deductible assumed not to change under USA and Flat Taxes.

## APPENDIX—*Continued*

### Dynamic Effect of Tax Restructuring Proposals on the Tax Treatment of R&D:  Example[18]

ASSUMPTIONS

| Foreign share of return | 50 percent |
|---|---|
| Foreign withholding tax | 5 percent |

| | Total | Qualified | Nonqualified |
|---|---|---|---|
| R&D expenses (section 174) | 100.00 | 42.00 | 58.00 |
| Wages and salaries | 52.00 | 22.00 | 30.00 |
| Employer share of payroll tax | 3.98 | NA | 3.98 |
| Employee benefits | 6.24 | NA | 6.24 |
| Fixed cost (depreciation) | 15.00 | NA | 15.00 |
| Other | 22.78 | 20.00 | 2.78 |
| U.S. R&D allocated to U.S. source | 75% | | |

| | Present Law | | Flat Tax | | USA Tax[a] |
|---|---|---|---|---|---|
| Item | Excess FTC | Deficit FTC | Armey-Shelby | Revenue neutral | Nunn-Domenici |
| Tax status | | | | | |
| Tax rate | 35% | 35% | 17% | 21% | 11% |
| Effective rate of R&D credit | 4.4% | 4.4% | NA | NA | NA |
| Foreign tax credit position | Excess | Deficit | NA | NA | NA |
| AMT | no | no | NA | NA | NA |
| Gross income | 90.68 | 98.15 | 103.11 | 103.27 | 102.56 |
| U.S. source | 45.34 | 49.08 | 51.56 | 51.64 | 51.28 |
| Foreign royalty, gross of withholding tax | 45.34 | 49.08 | 51.56 | 51.64 | 51.28 |
| Withholding tax | 2.27 | 2.45 | 2.58 | 2.58 | 2.56 |
| Research expense (sec. 174) | 100.00 | 100.00 | 100.00 | 100.00 | 100.00 |
| U.S. source | 75.00 | 75.00 | 100.00 | 100.00 | 100.00 |
| Foreign source | 25.00 | 25.00 | 0.00 | 0.00 | 0.00 |
| Components of research expense | | | | | |
| Wages | 52.00 | 52.00 | 52.00 | 52.00 | 52.00 |
| Payroll tax | 3.98 | 3.98 | 3.98 | 3.98 | 3.98 |
| Benefits | 6.24 | 6.24 | 6.24 | 6.24 | 6.24 |
| Capital cost recovery[b] | 15.00 | 15.00 | 16.86 | 16.86 | 16.86 |
| Other[c] | 22.78 | 22.78 | 22.78 | 22.78 | 22.78 |
| Qualified research expense | 42.00 | 42.00 | NA | NA | NA |
| Taxable income | −7.47 | 0.00 | 3.11 | 3.27 | −48.72 |
| U.S. tax before credits | −2.62 | 0.00 | 0.53 | 0.69 | 0.00 |
| Credits | 8.97 | 4.30 | 0.00 | 0.00 | 0.00 |
| Research credit | 1.85 | 1.85 | NA | NA | NA |
| Foreign tax credit | 7.12 | 2.45 | NA | NA | NA |
| Payroll tax credit | NA | NA | NA | NA | 0.00 |
| U.S. tax after credits | −11.58 | −4.30 | 0.53 | 0.69 | 0.00 |
| U.S. and foreign tax | −9.32 | −1.85 | 3.11 | 3.27 | 2.56 |
| Research expense after U.S. and foreign tax | 90.68 | 98.15 | 103.11 | 103.27 | 102.56 |

[a]USA Business Tax is assumed to be passed forward in prices.  Prices are shown net of USA Tax.
[b]R&D capital costs generally are five-year property under present law but would be expenses under a consumption tax. With 7% annual growth, steady-state ratio of depreciation to investment is 89%.
[c]Amount deductible assumed not to change under USA and Flat Taxes.

[18]Taxes imposed on compensation costs are assumed to be borne 100 percent by workers.

# 9

# U.S. Tax Policy and Multinational Corporations: Incentives, Problems, and Directions for Reform

R. GLENN HUBBARD[1]

*Columbia University and the National Bureau of Economic Research*

## INTRODUCTION

As multinational corporations play a larger role in the business activities of the global economy, interest in international aspects of capital income taxation has been stimulated. In the United States, debate has centered on the competitive position of U.S. firms in international product and capital markets. This concern is accompanied by complaints that U.S. international tax rules have become more complex and more distorting in the past several years, particularly since the passage of the Tax Reform Act of 1986. Discussions in Congress and the administration over the past several years indicate a willingness to consider significant reforms. In Europe, increased liberalization of capital markets prompted European Commission discussions on harmonization of corporate taxation. These policy developments around the world raise a deeper question of whether the current system of taxing international income is viable in a world of significant capital market integration and global commercial competition.

Academic researchers have shown renewed interest in the determinants of capital formation and allocation, patterns of finance in multinational companies, international competition, and opportunities for income shifting and tax avoidance. This research brings together approaches used by specialists in public finance and international economics.[2] In this chapter, I describe the objectives that guide the study of international tax rules and provide an introduction to U.S. tax

---

[1]The author is grateful to Thomas Barthold, Dale Jorgenson, Peter Merrill, and James Poterba for helpful comments and suggestions, and to the American Enterprise Institute for financial support.

[2]See, for example, the paper in Razin and Slemrod (1990); see also Giovannini et al. (1993); and Feldstein et al. (1995).

law. In addition, I analyze empirical evidence on investment and financing incentives created by U.S. international tax rules and consider possible reforms.[3] Finally, I describe how recent proposals for fundamental tax reform could affect multinational firms.

## TAX REFORM OBJECTIVES

To frame a discussion of international tax reform or any broad tax reform it is necessary to articulate the objectives clearly. This chapter considers three objectives—economic efficiency, competitiveness, and simplicity. Much of the debate over reform of international tax rules in the U.S. tax system stems from conflicts among these objectives.

### Economic Efficiency

The federal government in the United States must raise substantial revenue each year. Absent reliance on lump-sum taxes, policymakers must choose among tax instruments and definitions of the tax base that distort decisions about saving or investment or work, thereby contributing to a loss in economic efficiency. The framework for analyzing international tax rules should focus on how to structure a system with the least severe distortions, subject to raising revenue and other policy concerns.

Economists' exploration of "optimal taxation" has not always produced simple rules to guide the policy debate, but at least one clear statement has emerged since the pioneering work of Diamond and Mirrlees (1971). The tax system should attempt to preserve "production efficiency" even if it introduces other distortions.[4] This means that all firms should face the same prices for inputs, including for our purposes the cost of capital, and for output. The reason to encourage production efficiency can be understood by considering the consequences of its absence; production could be reallocated to achieve a greater output for a given level of input.

In the domestic context, broad-based income or consumption taxes are consistent with production efficiency. The term "broad-based income tax" is used here to denote one with a Haig-Simons definition of income and one in which there is full integration of the individual and the corporate income tax systems (U.S. Department of the Treasury, 1992a). Under such a regime, there is a wedge

---

[3]I do not address explicitly the question of whether incremental outbound foreign direct investment is "good" or "bad" for U.S. output or jobs. Economists have generally not taken seriously arguments that outbound foreign direct investment "destroys American jobs" (see, for example, Graham and Krugman, 1991; Feldstein, 1995; Lipsey, 1995).

[4]Conditions required to justify this result include, among other things, the availability of a variety of tax instruments and the ability to tax away pure profits.

between the cost of capital to businesses and the net rate of return received by individual savers, but because the wedge does not vary across firms, production efficiency is maintained. A "broad-based consumption tax" goes a step further. Not only is the cost of capital equivalent across firms, but also it equals the net rate of return to individual savers.

To think of production efficiency in a global economy in which capital is mobile across national boundaries, we should focus on worldwide production efficiency, wherever investments require the same risk-adjusted pretax rate of return, irrespective of the investment's location or the nationality of the owner or investor. This concept of production efficiency implies that worldwide output will be maximized for any given level of inputs; it is similar to arguments used to bolster the case for "free trade."

One way to achieve production efficiency in the international context is for all countries to adopt identical broad-based income or consumption taxes of the type described above. This adoption is not realistic, of course, nor is it necessary to achieve production efficiency. With full integration of corporate and individual income taxes, a pure residence-based tax system, in which a country's residents are taxed on all capital income they receive, would suffice. What would such a system look like? It would embody accrual taxation of the worldwide income of residents, offset with an unlimited credit for foreign taxes paid. In the real world, the temptation to tax capital owned by foreigners, together with the administration and monitoring problems associated with accrual taxation, explains the absence of such a prototype from the set of tax systems we see in practice.

Could a pure source-based or territorial tax system in which each country placed a uniform tax on all capital income generated domestically, irrespective of the owners of the capital (i.e., a flat-rate business tax with full integration of individual and corporate taxes), achieve production efficiency? Production efficiency could be achieved only in the unlikely event that all countries choose the identical effective tax rate on capital income. In addition, as elaborated later, a territorial system places significant pressure on rules governing the allocation of income and expenses, rules at the heart of many of the current debates over international tax reform.

## Competitiveness

Competitiveness is simply the ability of U.S.-headquartered firms to compete successfully with similarly situated foreign firms in international and domestic markets. This means that whatever else they do, U.S. international tax rules should not place a U.S. business at a competitive disadvantage in a foreign market, nor should they favor or penalize foreign or domestic businesses operating in the U.S. market. If effective tax rates on capital income were identical across countries, objectives of efficiency and competitiveness would always be compatible, but in practice the two objectives may be in conflict. For example, U.S. firms operating in low-tax countries abroad may be required to pay a "residual" tax in the United States in the name of efficiency, a tax that may place them at a disadvantage in competing with foreign multinationals in the low-tax jurisdiction.

Recently, some analysts have suggested that the focus of U.S. tax policy on production efficiency is misplaced when applied to multinational corporations (Frisch, 1990; Hufbauer, 1992). In this argument, if portfolio capital is perfectly mobile internationally, multinational firms do not play a crucial role as allocators of capital. That is, if foreign subsidies raise funds at the margin from selling debt and equity to owners of portfolio capital rather than from parent-provided equity, concerns about efficiency should focus on portfolio investment.[5] Moreover, if multinational enterprises exist to provide and coordinate "headquarters" services such as research and development or general management for related groups of firms and the location of these services generates spillovers in the home country, then concerns about the "competitiveness" of these firms in world markets should be discussed in tax policy debates.[6] In practice, these arguments are associated with proposals to exempt active foreign-source income from U.S. taxation.

## Simplicity

All else being equal, simple tax rules reduce compliance costs, facilitate tax administration, and limit the possibility of varying tax treatments of similarly situated firms. As such, a policy focus on "principled simplification" is likely to enhance both economic efficiency and competitiveness. The costs of compliance with international tax rules may pose serious efficiency and competitiveness concerns, and both business leaders and policymakers have voiced concern that the complexity of U.S. international rules increased after the passage of the Tax Reform Act of 1986.[7]

---

[5]The substitutability of direct and portfolio capital is an empirical question. Portfolio and direct investment involve an important *nontax* difference since direct investment offers both ownership and control, as opposed to only ownership in the case of portfolio investment. The empirical investigation of Gordon and Jun (1993) does not find tax factors to be the most prominent determinant of the mix between direct and portfolio investment. More empirical study is needed to assess the relative roles of multinational firms' investment and portfolio investment in allocating capital for business investment.

[6]The arguments that high value-added "headquarters" investments such as R&D generate externalities for the headquarters country is not *per se* a justification for a territorial tax system to avoid placing a residual tax on multinational firms' investment income. To the extent that headquarters activities generate externalities, they should be subsidized directly and generally. If, for example, the present subsidy to R&D in the United States is "too low," it could be increased across the board. It is unlikely that changing the tax rate on multinational firms headquartered in the United States is the most efficient means of achieving the appropriate subsidy.

[7]Proposals for simplification have been offered in U.S. Department of the Treasury (1993).

## Conflicts Among Objectives

Conflicts between policy objectives of efficiency and competitiveness typically arise in debates over the appropriate norms for international tax policy. Derived from models of international trade and capital income taxation, two principles are conventionally suggested as guides to the taxation of international investment:

1. Capital-Export Neutrality: Investors should pay equivalent taxes on capital income, regardless of the county in which that income is earned.
2. Capital-Import Neutrality: All investments within a country should face the same tax burden, regardless of the nationality of the investor.

As noted earlier, satisfying both principles at the same time is possible only if effective tax rates on capital income are identical across countries.[8]

The U.S. Treasury Department has generally favored the norm of capital-export neutrality,[9] with a system that taxes the worldwide income of resident multinational firms and provides a tax credit for taxes on foreign-source income paid abroad.[10] However, concern over preservation of the U.S. tax base has led to complex rules, reducing the likelihood of achieving efficiency, competitiveness, and simplicity objectives.[11]

## U.S. INTERNATIONAL TAX RULES: THE INCENTIVES

Incentives in U.S. international tax rules are considered here in three parts: (1) basic rules for determining U.S. tax treatment of foreign-source income, (2) complications of those basic rules arising from provisions of the alternative mini-

---

[8]Economic analysis of the relative merits of norms of capital-export neutrality (CEN) and capital-import neutrality (CIN) has traditionally compared distortions in the *level* of saving within an economy and in the *allocation* of that saving among alternative investments at home and abroad. Implementing CIN by exempting active foreign-source income from taxation can promote worldwide economic efficiency if domestic savings are inefficiently low, although other capital tax instruments may also be used to achieve this objective. By contrast, CEN promotes worldwide efficiency in the allocation of savings. As such, CEN may be a better guiding principle when efficiency costs in the allocation of savings are large relative to costs of tax-induced distortions in the level of savings (see, for example, Horst, 1980; Giovannini, 1989). Indeed, empirical evidence generally supports the proportion that the responsiveness of domestic saving to a change in the net return is less then the responsiveness of the allocation of investment to tax policy. Nevertheless, some compromise between CEN and CIN is both inevitable and unobjectionable given the presence of tax-induced distortions of both investment and saving decisions and the complexity of the modern multinational firm.

[9]See, for example, the discussion in Hufbauer (1992).

[10]In practice, the U.S. system departs significantly from CEN, in part because of the absence of accrual taxation of foreign-source income and limitations on the foreign tax credit.

[11]For example, multinational enterprises often complain that policymakers' pursuit of CEN is at the expense of U.S. firms' competitiveness since, in some cases, U.S. firms may face a higher total tax burden on foreign-source income than foreign competitors.

mum tax, and (3) rules relating to the allocation of expenses related to interest and to research and development.[12]

## Taxation of Foreign-Source Income: The Basics

The United States claims tax authority over all residents, meaning that U.S. individuals and corporations must pay tax to the U.S. government on all their income, whether earned in the United States or abroad.[13] As noted earlier, "residence" is not the only possible basis for tax authority; some countries tax their residents on a "territorial" basis, so that only income earned within the country's borders is subject to tax.

In addition to potential U.S. tax liabilities, U.S. multinationals usually owe taxes to foreign governments on profits earned within their borders. To avoid double taxation of foreign-source income, U.S. tax law provides a foreign tax credit for income and related taxes paid to foreign governments. For example, in the simplest possible situation, a U.S. corporation earning $100 in a foreign country with a 10 percent tax rate (a foreign tax obligation of $10) pays only $25 to the U.S. government since its U.S. corporate tax obligation of $35 (35 percent of $100) is reduced to $25 by the foreign tax credit of $10. The foreign tax credit is, however, limited to the equivalent U.S. tax liability on that income. If the foreign tax rate is 50 percent instead, the firm pays $50 to the foreign government, but its U.S. foreign tax credit is limited to $35. Hence, a U.S. firm receives full tax credits for foreign tax payments paid only when it is in an "excess limit" position, that is, when its average foreign tax rate is less than the average tax imposed by the United States on foreign-source income. A firm has "excess credits" if its available foreign tax credits are greater than its U.S. tax liability on its foreign-source income. U.S. firms are required to calculate their foreign tax credits on a worldwide basis, so that all foreign income and foreign taxes paid are added together in computation of the foreign tax credit limit. Income is also decomposed into different functional "baskets" in the calculation of applicable credits and limits.

Deferral of U.S. taxation of certain foreign earnings is another important feature of the U.S. system for taxing overseas income. This deferral is of two types. The first is simply that unrealized capital gains are usually not taxed, a general feature of most income tax systems. Second, earnings of foreign subsidiaries of U.S. corporations are not subject to U.S. taxation until repatriated to their parent corporations. This type of deferral is available only to foreign operations that are incorporated separately in foreign countries ("subsidiaries" of the

---

[12]This is, of course, not an exhaustive list, which could include an analysis of transfer pricing regulations, sales source rules, foreign sales corporation rules, and other provisions.

[13]For more detailed descriptions of systems for taxing income from foreign direct investments, see Ault and Bradford (1990); Frisch (1990); Hines and Hubbard (1990); U.S. Congress, Joint Committee on Taxation (1990, 1991); and U.S. Department of the Treasury (1993).

parent) and not to consolidated ("branch") operations. Multinational companies generally are able to choose the organizational form of overseas operations and thereby influence their tax obligations. On the one hand, U.S. parent firms are generally taxed on their subsidiaries' foreign income only when it is repatriated and receive "indirect' foreign tax credits ("deemed-paid credits") for subsidiary foreign income taxes paid on income subsequently received as dividends. On the other hand, the U.S. government taxes branch profits as they are earned, just as it would profits earned within the United States. Organizing as a branch nevertheless offers the chance to deduct foreign branch losses from U.S. income and may involve more lenient foreign regulations.

It is possible for deferral to encourage firms facing low foreign tax rates to delay the repatriation of dividends.[14,15] This incentive is enhanced when firms expect that future years offer a more favorable tax climate for repatriation, for example, in anticipation of a reduction in the domestic corporate income tax rate on excess foreign tax credits to use in offsetting U.S. tax liability on repatriations. Available empirical evidence suggests that firms choose patterns of dividend repatriations to minimize tax liability (see Hines and Hubbard, 1990; Altshuler et al., 1995).

Dividends to the parent company are not the only possible form of repatriation.[16] Interest paid to the parent to service debt capital contributions is generally deductible in the host country. In some cases, transfer pricing can be used by a subsidiary to shift income to the parent or to other subsidiaries of the parent having more favorable tax treatment. Royalty payments to the parent can serve a similar function. Foreign governments often impose withholding taxes, creditable against foreign tax liability of the parent, on dividend, interest, rent, and royalty payments from foreign subsidiaries to U.S. parents.

## Alternative Minimum Tax Complications

As it does in the domestic context, the alternative minimum tax (AMT) embodies incentives affecting investment and financial policy decisions of multina-

---

[14]Deferral *per se* may not encourage firms to delay paying dividends from foreign subsidiaries, since the tax to the U.S. government must at some point be paid (see Hartman, 1985; Altshuler and Fulghieri, 1994; Cummins and Hubbard, 1995).

[15]Congress enacted the subpart F provisions in 1962 in an attempt to prevent indefinite deferral of U.S. tax liability on foreign-source income. These provisions apply to "controlled foreign corporations" at least 50 percent owned by U.S. persons holding stakes of at least 10 percent each. Subpart F provisions treat passive income as if it had been distributed to the U.S. parent company, thereby subjecting it to current taxation. Controlled foreign corporations that reinvest their earnings in active foreign businesses sidestep subpart F rules and may continue to defer U.S. tax liability on those earnings. Subpart F coverage was expanded in the Tax Reform Act of 1986 (see discussion in U.S. Department of the Treasury, 1993).

[16]For a comparison of the tax treatment of alternative forms of repatriation, see Hines and Hubbard (1990).

tional firms.[17] First, foreign tax credit calculations differ between the regular tax and the AMT.[18] Second, relative investment incentives for regular tax and AMT firms differ from those in the domestic setting. The tax code often penalizes new domestic investment undertaken by an AMT firm relative to investment undertaken by a firm subject to the regular tax (see, for example, Lyon, 1990; Prakken, 1994). A multinational firm, however, claims the same deductions for depreciation of foreign-use property under the AMT as under the regular tax.[19] Therefore the AMT may create a *relative* incentive to locate investment overseas. Incentives for domestic investment are reduced by the AMT, whereas incentives for equity-financed foreign investment are unchanged or even improved under the AMT[20] (see Lyon and Silverstein, 1995). The AMT may also offer parent firms the opportunity to receive dividends from subsidiaries at a cost lower than that possible under the regular tax (see, again, Lyon and Silverstein, 1995).

## Allocation of Interest and R&D Expenses

### Interest Allocation Rules

In the domestic context, interest expense is deductible against taxable income; corporations can carry back net operating losses for three years and, to avail themselves of deductibility, carry them forward for 15 years. Determining interest deductions for multinational corporations is more complicated. The spirit of U.S. rules for the allocation of interest deductions is to allow the deductibility of interest against taxable income in the United States only for interest expense generating income subject to taxation in the United States. Such an approach is inherently difficult to implement because of the fungibility of funds within a multinational firm.

The regulatory distinction between "domestic" and "foreign" interest expense is not merely academic and can affect firms' costs of finance. When interest

---

[17]It is probably important to analyze the interaction of AMT and foreign tax rules. In 1990, 53 percent of the assets and 56 percent of the foreign-source income of corporations filing Form 1118 could be attributed to firms paying AMT.

[18]The concepts of "worldwide income," "foreign income," and "U.S. tax liability" are calculated using AMT rules rather than regular tax rules. In addition, the combined use of AMT foreign tax credits and net operating loss deductions may not decrease tentative minimum tax by more then 90 percent. Such credits denied are treated like other excess foreign tax credits and may be carried back for two years and forward for five years to offset tentative minimum tax.

[19]Foreign investment receives slower depreciation allowances *absolutely* than domestic investment under both the regular tax and the AMT systems. Firms subject to the AMT may nonetheless face a *relative* incentive to invest overseas.

[20]With *debt* finance, incentives for foreign and domestic investment may be curtailed by the AMT. This is because the after-tax cost of $1.00 of interest expense increases from $0.65 under the regular tax to $0.80 under the AMT. Nonetheless, although the cost of all debt-financed investment is raised under the AMT, the cost of foreign investment relative to domestic investment is still lower for the AMT firm than for the regular tax firm (see Lyon and Silverstein, 1995).

expense is determined to be foreign, it reduces foreign taxable income but only for the purposes of U.S. taxation, since foreign governments do not as a rule allow U.S. firms to lower foreign taxable income because of interest expenses in the United States. As a result, a U.S. firm benefits from interest deductions determined to be "foreign" only if that firm is in an excess limit position for foreign tax credit purposes. This occurs because, for such firms, a portion of the foreign-source income is subject to residual tax; incremental interest expense allocated to foreign-source income simply reduces U.S. taxable income for the firm one for one. For firms with excess credits, the interest allocation rules can lead, in effect, to a partial disallowance of interest deductions.

The Tax Reform Act of 1986 adopted a "one-taxpayer rule" in which the characteristics of all members of a controlled group determined interest allocation. Prior to 1986, interest expenses were arrived at for each company individually within a controlled group. The assumption underlying the new rule is that fungibility of funds implies that borrowing should be evaluated at the level of a controlled group. In practice, firms are obligated to allocate interest expense on the basis of the book values of domestic and foreign assets. As a consequence, firms with substantial foreign assets relative to total assets and with excess foreign tax credits were unable to deduct a portion of their interest expense after 1986. Whether this denial raises firms' cost of capital depends on the cost at which firms can substitute equity for debt finance.

## R&D Allocation Rules

Given the role often attributed to R&D intangible capital in explaining economic performance, it is not surprising that business, academic, and public policy attention has also focused on the tax treatment of R&D. In the domestic context, corporate R&D expenses are treated favorably for tax purposes.[21] As with interest expenses, U.S. multinationals generally are not allowed to deduct their entire U.S. expenses on R&D against domestic taxable income; such expenses are allocated between domestic- and foreign-source income. The rules' intent is to preserve the favorable treatment of R&D only for expenditures related to production for domestic markets.

As with interest expenses, the allocation of R&D expenses between domestic and foreign incomes can affect the value of the deduction. R&D expenses allocated against foreign-source income are valued by a U.S. firm only if it is in an excess limit position for foreign tax credit purposes. The Treasury Department

---

[21]Such expenses are deductible for tax purposes, receiving favorable tax treatment given that accumulated R&D is usually thought of as a capital good. Since 1981, the United States has also had a research and experimentation (R&E) tax credit. The Tax Reform Act of 1986 reduced the generosity of this tax credit to 20 percent for eligible incremental R&D expenses above a base equal to the average of the firm's prior three years' worth of spending on R&D. After 1986, the credit survived through a series of temporary extensions.

formalized rules for R&D expense allocation (section 1.861-8) in 1977. Over the course of the 1980s and 1990s, these rules have been changed many times.[22]

## EFFECTS OF TAX INCENTIVES ON COST OF
## CAPITAL AND INVESTMENT

Having identified some key investment and financing incentives present in U.S. international tax rules, let us turn now to empirical evidence on the effects of thee incentives on the cost of capital faced by U.S. multinational firms.

Existing empirical studies of determinants of foreign direct investment (FDI) reflect researchers' interest in either industrial organization or taxation. Industrial organization inquiries have generally ignored tax considerations and analyzed FDI as being governed by firms' desire to exploit the value of ownership-specific assets (e.g., intangible capital) or location-specific advantages related to sourcing or marketing.[23]

Empirical research has analyzed the roles played by ownership-specific and location-specific variables in determining FDI. Public finance inquiries have focused on the role of differential tax treatment in determining the source and location of FDI, holding nontax determinants constant. In this vein, a significant body of empirical research has examined the effects of taxation on the cost of capital for FDI into the United States, primarily the simple relationship between capital flows and measures of after-tax rates of return or effective tax rates on capital income.

Following work by Hartman (1984, 1985), several studies have used annual aggregate data for inbound FDI financed by subsidiary earnings and parent company transfers of funds. Hartman's approach assumes that subsidiaries' dividend payouts are a residual in firm decisions. Payout ratios do not affect firms' required rate of return on equity invested, and permanent changes in home country tax rates do not affect dividend payouts or the cost of capital. In the context of FDI, these implications permit Hartman and others to ignore effects of permanent changes in home country tax parameters on FDI in "mature" subsidiaries paying dividends to their parent firms.[24]

Hartman estimates the effects on U.S. inbound FDI of changes in the after-tax rates of return received by foreign investors in U.S. inbound FDI and by

---

[22]Significant modifications were made in the Economic Recovery Tax Act of 1981, Tax Reform Act of 1986, Technical and Miscellaneous Revenue Act of 1988, Omnibus Budget Reconciliation Act of 1984, and subsequent legislative and administrative extensions. See Hines (1993) for a detailed discussion.

[23]See, for example, the reviews of studies in Caves (1982).

[24]This approach is more suitably applied to firm-level data. The underlying model suggests that a mature subsidiary's investment financed by retained earnings is unaffected by the home country tax rate. This suggestion is not equivalent to a claim that aggregate investment out of retained earnings will not be affected by the home country tax rate.

investors in U.S. capital generally, with the intent of measuring impacts of shifts in returns to new FDI. He finds that the ratio of FDI to GNP (gross national product) increases as after-tax rates of return rise and decreases as the relative tax rate on foreigners rises. These results suggested that taxes are an important determinant of FDI, and Hartman's study prompted many subsequent rounds of replication and refinement (see, for example, Boskin and Gale, 1987; Newlon, 1987; Slemrod, 1990).

These studies advance our understanding of the effects of taxation on FDI but raise a number of concerns. An obvious concern relates to problems of inference about tax effects on *firms'* decisions using such highly aggregated data. A second concern is that nontax determinants of FDI are not modeled. Third, the FDI data supplied by the Bureau of Economic Analysis suffer two drawbacks: (1) they measure financial flows rather than new capital investment *per se*, and (2) they are based on periodic benchmark surveys, raising the possibility that FDI flows are more mismeasured the further the observation is from a benchmark year.

In a world of ideal data, assessing the impact of taxation on firms' cost of capital for FDI would be straightforward. Consider a U.S. parent firm deciding how much to invest in a particular country. Intuitively, neoclassical models of investment predict that the firm will invest until the value of an additional dollar of capital equals the cost of investing.[25] Unfortunately, this benchmark approach is not particularly useful as a practical guide to estimating the effects of taxation on the levels of firms' FDI. First, it is difficult to develop a proxy for the incremental value of investing from available data on financial market valuation even under the best of circumstances. For FDI, a further complication arises because location-specific effects on the value of incremental investment in the subsidiary cannot be captured by using available financial data at the parent-firm level, and subsidiary-specific financial market data are, of course, not observable.

To reduce these practical problems, Cummins and Hubbard (1995) employ an empirical approach developed to estimate effects of after-tax returns to investing with fewer informational requirements than conventional models. It allows one to ask the question: Given a change in a tax parameter, how does a subsidiary's return to investing change, and how does FDI change?

Tax considerations can affect subsidiaries' new capital investment decisions through two channels.[26] First, host country corporate income tax rates, investment incentives, and depreciation rules affect the cost of capital for foreign investors. This channel has been the focus of empirical analysis of the effects of tax policy on domestic investment. A second channel through which tax policy affects FDI from countries with worldwide tax systems such as the United States is

---

[25]See, for example, Alworth (1988).

[26]In general, investment through acquisitions is governed by a different set of tax determinants. See, for example, the discussion in Auerbach and Hassett (1993).

through variation over time and across firms in the "tax price" of subsidiaries' dividend repatriations to their parent firms. In the method used by Cummins and Hubbard (1995), subsidiary dividend decisions and the cost of capital are not affected by permanent changes in the tax price of repatriations, although temporary changes can affect both repatriations and FDI.[27]

In this channel, there are two sources of variation in the tax price of dividend repatriations. The first reflects variation over time in host and home country statutory corporate income tax rates. The second reflects variation in foreign tax credit status (i.e., excess credit or excess limit positions) both across firms and over time for a given firm. Parents in an excess limit position owe residual U.S. corporate tax if the U.S. corporate tax rate exceeds the applicable foreign tax rate. Parents in an excess credit position owe no residual U.S. corporate tax.

Cummins and Hubbard (1995) analyze effects of changes in pretax returns to investing and in the tax parameters described above on FDI by U.S. multinational firms. Using panel data on investment from 282 to 632 U.S. subsidiaries from 1980 through 1991 in Canada, the United Kingdom, Germany, France, Australia, and Japan, they test the hypothesis that host and home country tax parameters should be included in the model and estimate the responsiveness of subsidiary investment to pretax returns and tax parameters.[28]

The results of these tests reject conclusively the simple notion that "taxes don't matter." On the contrary, both host country and domestic tax parameters should be included in the correct specification of the subsidiary's investment model. The estimated responsiveness of firm-level FDI to the tax-adjusted cost of capital is statistically and economically significant. Each increase of 1 per-

---

[27]The Cummins-Hubbard study works within a framework known as the "trapped equity" or "tax capitalization" view of corporate dividends. A simple example illustrates this view. Suppose that a parent firm capitalizes a wholly owned subsidiary with an intitial transfer of equity capital. When the subsidiary has growth opportunities and desired investment exceeds internally generated funds, the parent transfers additional funds to it. For a mature subsidiary, equity is "trapped"; earnings exceed profitable investment opportunities, and the subsidiary repatriates the residual funds. Costly repatriation can be delayed as long as the subsidiary has active investment opportunities abroad, but once these are exhausted, subpart F rules prevent the use of passive investments to defer U.S. tax obligation. In this trapped equity view, subsidiary dividend payouts are unaffected by permanent changes in their tax price. Although this view is controversial in the context of dividend payouts from a domestic firm to its shareholders owing to potential information or corporate control problems, it is arguably less controversial in the application to dividends paid by majority or wholly owned subsidiaries to their parent firms.

[28]The data set is constructed from the Compustat Geographic Segment file. (Geographic Segment disclosures are mandated by *Statement of Financial Accounting Standards No. 14—Financial Reporting of Segments in a Business Enterprise*, issued in 1976.) Both U.S.- and foreign-incorporated firms report sales, operating income, and fixed assets. Geographic regions are reported for seven years at a time. Cummins and Hubbard combine two seven-year panels to obtain a data set on outbound FDI by U.S. multinationals over the period extending from 1980 through 1991. Although the number of subsidiaries reporting information varies from year to year (generally growing over the period), the study obtained information from 282 to 632 U.S. foreign subsidiaries.

centage point in the cost of capital leads to a 1 to 2 percent decrease in the subsidiary's annual rate of investment (annual investment divided by beginning-of-year capital stock).[29]

Some examples illustrating this finding are instructive. As noted earlier, tax parameters can affect the cost of capital for FDI through host country and domestic channels. First, increases in the availability in the host country of investment incentives such as investment tax credits or accelerated depreciation reduce the cost of capital and stimulate FDI. Second, temporary changes in U.S. statutory corporate tax rates or parent firms' foreign tax credit positions affect the cost of capital and FDI. If, for example, a parent firm expects to move from an excess limit position to an excess credit position, its cost of capital rises relative to a parent firm with no change in foreign tax credit status if its investments are in high-tax jurisdictions, leading the firm to reduce its FDI.[30]

### Efficiency, Competitiveness, and Simplicity Concerns

The findings in Cummins and Hubbard (1995) are consistent with the hypothesis that permanent changes in the tax price of subsidiary dividend repatriations do not affect the cost of capital for investment by dividend-paying subsidiaries. This result permits some observations about the extent to which the U.S. system of taxing multinationals' income corresponds to norms of capital-export neutrality or capital-import neutrality. Hartman (1985) and others have noted that for dividend-paying subsidiaries, permanent changes in the home country (for our purposes, the United States) corporate tax rate should have no effect on FDI financed out of subsidiary retained earnings—a capital-import neutral result for these firms. This finding does not carry over precisely to the Cummins-Hubbard framework, because changes in the parent firm's foreign tax credit status also affect the tax price of repatriations.[31] With expected changes in foreign tax credit status, capital-export neutrality, capital-import neutrality, or neither may hold. Similar examples can be constructed for "immature" subsidiaries financing initial investment using parent equity transfers. To summarize, the U.S. tax system creates potentially complex effects of tax parameters on overseas investment decisions, and these effects can vary significantly across firms. It is difficult to reconcile such patterns with an economic efficiency goal.

Since evidence suggests that the U.S. tax system can affect the cost of capital for and investment by U.S. multinational firms, an important concern is competi-

---

[29]These estimates are broadly consistent with those reported for firm-level business fixed investment in the United States (see Cummins, et al., 1994, 1996) and with those for firm-level domestic fixed investment in European countries (see Cummins, et al., 1995).

[30]This assumes that the subsidiaries are repatriating dividends to the parent in current and future periods.

[31]Hartman's result holds in the case for which the parent's foreign tax credit position is not expected to change.

tiveness. If U.S. firms are subject to a residual U.S. tax on investments in low-tax foreign countries, will they not be at a disadvantage in competing with multinationals headquartered in other countries?[32]

The answer is perhaps. Although it is true that the present system imposes a tax penalty on U.S. multinationals whose overseas operations are largely in low-tax countries, empirical studies of subsidiaries' dividend repatriations have shown that at least prior to the Tax Reform Act of 1986, significant "cross-crediting" of high-tax and low-tax income occurred (see Hines and Hubbard, 1990; Altshuler and Newlon, 1993; Altshuler et al., 1995). Firms with low-tax subsidiaries could blend repatriations from such subsidiaries with repatriations from high-tax subsidiaries. The Tax Reform Act of 1986 restricted the use of cross-crediting by increasing the number of separate limitation baskets. As a result, it is possible that the cost of capital faced by U.S. firms' subsidiaries operating in relatively low-tax jurisdictions rose after 1986.[33] Because the new limitation baskets apply to only about one-fourth of all foreign-source income (U.S. Department of the Treasury, 1993), it is worth asking whether much revenue is, in fact, being protected at the cost of the more complex rules. Unfortunately, at least to my knowledge, there has been no comprehensive analysis of repatriation decisions using data after 1986. Such an inquiry would require an examination of corporate tax return data on the post-1986 period by the Joint Committee on Taxation or the Office of Tax Analysis.

In a separate exercise, Grubert and Mutti (1994), using tax return data for 1990, have estimated that the average effective U.S. tax rate on active foreign income is approximately zero, although some individual firms, of course, pay residual U.S. tax.[34] This estimate reflects the ability of firms operating in both low-tax and high-tax jurisdictions to adopt repatriation strategies to minimize the residual tax.[35] In addition, Grubert and Mutti note that in some cases, subsidiaries of U.S. firms repatriate low-taxed royalty and interest income along with more highly taxed dividend income. If the United States had a territorial (exemption)

---

[32]Calculations by the Organization for Economic Cooperation and Development (1991) and Jun (1995) suggest that for equity-financed investments, U.S. firms often face a higher cost of capital for overseas investment than non-U.S. firms.

[33]Since passage of the Tax Reform Act of 1986, section 904(d) of the Internal Revenue Code specifies separate foreign tax credit limitation for eight types of income. Other types of income are subject to a common "general limitation."

[34]The usual caution against interpreting the Grubert-Mutti calculation as a "revenue estimate" is in order. They assume no significant behavioral response by firms if the United States were to switch from a worldwide to a territorial tax system. This presumes, among other things, that firms would be unable to reclassify "royalties" as "dividends."

[35]The Grubert-Mutti calculations do not incorporate effects of the AMT. As noted earlier, the impact of the AMT is difficult to gauge. On the one hand, if the firm has domestic losses and significant foreign income, it may be subject to the 90 percent limitation on the foreign tax credit. On the other hand, if the firm is subject to the AMT because of domestic considerations, the residual tax rate is only 20 percent.

tax system, dividend income would be exempt in their estimate whereas world-wide taxation with a foreign tax credit would still apply to royalty income.

The U.S. Treasury Department's interim study of U.S. international tax rules identified "simplicity" as an important goal for reform. This emphasis does not seem misplaced. The Office of Tax Policy Research at the University of Michigan has been compiling information on the overall costs of tax compliance for large corporations. Blumenthal and Slemrod (1994) analyzed compliance costs for 365 firms, with an emphasis on studying costs associated with taxing foreign-source income. They report that 39 percent of the total compliance cost of federal taxes can be traced to foreign-source income. Since the average fractions of assets abroad (19.2 percent), sales abroad (21.3 percent), or employment abroad (16.6 percent) are less then 39 percent, compliance costs associated with foreign-source income are about 8.5 percent of net U.S. revenue raised. The Blumenthal-Slemrod survey identifies foreign tax credit rules, expense allocation rules, and transfer pricing rules as being most burdensome.

Compliance burdens for U.S. multinational firms occur within the U.S. system of worldwide taxation. The Grubert-Mutti estimate suggests that the United States raises very little revenue from this system. Should we infer, then, that the United States should switch from a worldwide to a territorial tax system? Again, the answer is only perhaps. Although either system provides relief from double taxation and a territorial system may in some ways be less expensive to administer, a move to a territorial system would significantly increase pressure on transfer pricing and allocation rules to address potential income shifting.[36] In addition, a territorial system might lead to an expansion of tax-haven activity and erosion of the tax base.[37] To shed light on this concern, researchers and the Treasury Department should examine the experience of France and the Netherlands with territorial systems.

## Complications from the Alternative Minimum Tax

Empirical evidence on incentive effects of the AMT is not abundant, though the significant stock of outstanding corporate AMT credits indicates the potential importance of these effects (see Gerardi et al., 1994). The incentive effects of AMT-related international tax rules on domestic investment are ambiguous. On the one hand, recall that the AMT can in some cases create a relative incentive to investment abroad rather than domestically for firms subject to the AMT. Calculations reported in Lyon and Silverstein (1995) document this relative incentive

---

[36]For empirical evidence on the significant potential for income shifting, see Harris et al. (1993); and Hines and Rice (1994).

[37]Indeed, the territorial system ("modified exemption") prototype discussed in U.S. Department of the Treasury (1993) would exempt high-tax active foreign-source income. The study noted the pressure that such a system would place on source and expense allocation rules because classifying an expense as relating to exempt income would be tantamount to denying a deduction for the expense.

in the case of equity-financed investment.[38] On the other hand, AMT provisions may offer a window of opportunity for repatriating overseas earnings at a lower cost than that under the regular tax. To the extent that repatriated earnings are retained by U.S. parent firms, these incentives offer an ambiguous effect on overall domestic investment. Additional empirical analysis is needed to understand the incentive effects of the AMT.

### Allocation of Interest and R&D Expenses

As noted earlier, features of the current rules for allocating expenses for interest and R&D can in some cases lead to a partial disallowance of deductions, frustrating the law's intention of deductibility and leading to overtaxation of economic income. The available empirical evidence on these effects is summarized below.

In the case of interest allocation rules, it is possible that firms in an excess credit position with significant foreign assets do not receive the complete benefit of the interest deduction. As a result, the introduction of allocation rules would raise the cost of capital for such firms to the extent that they could not easily substitute equity for debt finance.[39] A simple test would be to compare investment before and after 1986 for firms in excess limit and excess credit positions, holding other determinants of investment constant. Using Compustat data on 203 firms, Froot and Hines (1994) control for industry effects and the importance of foreign assets. They find that from 1986 to 1991, firms that could not fully deduct their U.S. interest expenses on average both borrowed 4.2 percent less as a fraction of firm assets and invested 3.5 percent less in property, plant, and equipment than firms whose deductions were not affected by the interest allocation rules. In a careful analysis of 13 large U.S. nonfinancial multinational firms, Altshuler and Mintz (1995) found that the interest allocation rules raised the cost of debt finance significantly for domestic and foreign investment by U.S. firms with excess foreign tax credits.

Allocation rules for R&D expenses raise similar concerns for firms with excess foreign tax credits. Hines (1993), analyzing longitudinal data on 116 U.S. multinational firms in the Compustat data, argues that the elasticity of domestic

---

[38]Lyon and Silverstein calculated the magnitude of the change in the price of foreign investment relative to domestic investment between AMT and regular tax firms under a set of assumptions. Consider the case of equity-financed investments by firms in excess limit status for foreign tax credit purposes. Firms expecting to be subject to the AMT for 10 years face roughly equivalent effective tax rates for domestic and foreign-use equipment, whereas regular tax firms face significantly higher effective tax rates for foreign investment than for domestic investment. In the cases Lyon and Silverstein considered, foreign investment is treated less favorably than domestic investment for firms facing a given tax system. Nonetheless, the AMT creates a relative incentive to locate investment abroad rather than in the United States.

[39]For example, such firms could replace debt with preferred stock (Collins and Shackleford, 1992).

R&D spending with respect to the after-tax price of R&D is in the range of −1.2 to −1.6. Although these very high estimates of responsiveness of R&D to tax policy are controversial,[40] it is worth noting that Hines' estimates imply a large increase in R&D performed in the United States should R&D expense be 100 percent deductible against U.S. taxes. Evaluation of such reforms depends, of course, on the revenue cost and the availability of other means of stimulating R&D investment.

## INCREMENTAL REFORMS

Tax-induced differences in costs of funds across firms for similar investment projects are not the hallmark of an efficient tax system. Similarly, to the extent that our international tax rules do not permit full deductibility of expenses, U.S. firms are placed at a competitive disadvantage vis-á-vis firms headquartered elsewhere. Finally, even this cursory discussion of rules associated with expense allocation and the AMT makes it clear that sacrifices in economic efficiency and competitiveness in our current rules are not purchasing "simplicity."

What incremental reforms are suggested by these concerns? Let us put aside the question of the AMT, which is questionable tax policy warranting a more general discussion even in a strictly domestic context. With respect to interest allocation rules, the Tax Reform Act of 1986 applied a "water's-edge fungibility" approach.[41] In principle, "worldwide fungibility" could be implemented by combining domestic and foreign affiliates' interest expense and apportioning this combined amount to the income of the group by assets of domestic and foreign group members. In practice, this strategy is difficult to implement because of deferral. Alternatively, the United States could employ a simple "netting rule": interest would be allocated if the debt-asset ratio of the parent firm exceeded the debt-asset ratio of foreign subsidiaries or, possibly, the debt-asset ratio of the parent firm and foreign affiliates on a consolidated basis.[42] In this case, a U.S. parent firm would be permitted full deductibility of interest expense if its debt-asset ratio is no greater than that of its foreign subsidiaries. The usefulness of such a rule in mitigating problems under current law depends on the ease with which multinationals can lever assets in source countries. Another alternative would be a simple requirement that the U.S. parent have a specified minimum amount of equity relative to assets;[43] if more debt is used, a fraction of the interest expense would not be permitted.

---

[40]See the discussion in Hall (1993).

[41]Under a water's-edge approach, the debt of a U.S. parent is treated as if it supported foreign subsidiary investment to the same extent as domestic investment. Under a worldwide fungibility approach, a U.S. parent is allowed to take into account foreign subsidiaries' interest expense in apportioning its own interest expense.

[42]Some netting rules are discussed in Hufbauer (1992).

[43]Altshuler and Mintz (1995) refer to such a concept as a "fat capitalization" rule.

It is also possible to apply a worldwide fungibility approach to the allocation of expenses for R&D. As with borrowing, under such an approach, R&D expenses of foreign subsidiaries would be considered in the determination of whether to allocate some portion of U.S.-incurred R&D expense to foreign-source income. The case for such a policy change would be bolstered by empirical evidence supporting the notion that R&D within a multinational firm is done predominantly in locations in which related products are sold.

## ISSUES FOR GENERAL REFORM

The financing and investment incentives created by U.S. international tax rules are complex and in some cases difficult to measure. Against such a backdrop, it is not likely that simple general reforms will address the concerns of policymakers and the business community regarding efficiency, competitiveness, and simplicity. It is productive to examine reforms in two steps: first, incremental changes to reduce significant problems or anomalies under current law, and second, to consider "international tax reform" in the context of reform of capital taxation.[44]

As a first step it is possible to reduce violations of efficiency and competitiveness goals by modifying interest allocation rules and R&D allocation rules. Moreover, substantial simplification of foreign tax credit rules may be possible even in the context of the current worldwide tax system with deferral (see, for example, U.S. Department of the Treasury, 1993). Finally, simplification generally may be facilitated by international coordination, since many rules are designed to limit shifting of expenses or income for the purpose of tax avoidance. The form of this coordination should reflect the relative responsiveness to variation in tax rates of real investment and reported income. To the extent that the responsiveness of reported income is greater than that of real investment, policymakers may wish to focus on harmonizing statutory corporate tax rates while allowing investment incentives to vary across countries.

The broader issue of whether the United States should move closer to a pure worldwide tax system, for example, by eliminating deferral, or to a territorial (exemption) system should be considered in the context of broader tax policy decisions. For example, to the extent that corporate income taxation is viewed as a backstop against income shifting (as in Gordon and MacKie-Mason, 1995), a move to a territorial tax system may lead to an erosion of the U.S. domestic tax base and require offsets from other distorting taxes.

---

[44]Unfortunately, policymakers have not generally considered international tax reform in the context of general tax reform. For example, the Tax Reform Act of 1986 arguably used international tax rule changes to raise revenue rather than to advance the general goals of reform. The Clinton administration's initial 1993 budget package likewise focused on revenue enhancement in the international tax area.

Nonetheless, the broader tax reforms currently under current discussion suggest that a move to a territorial tax system should be taken seriously. Many reforms of business taxation, ranging from corporate tax integration to the adoption of consumption taxes, would be consistent with a territorial approach to the taxation of foreign-source income. As an illustration, the Treasury Department's proposal in 1992 for corporate tax integration incorporated a dividend exclusion prototype in which investors would not pay taxes on dividends received (see U.S. Department of the Treasury, 1992a, 1992b). The proposal might encourage examination of a modified exemption system under which U.S. parent firms would exclude from taxable income dividends received from overseas subsidiaries. The Treasury Department also described a Comprehensive Business Income Tax (CBIT) in which neither interest nor dividends would be deductible and in which investors would not pay taxes on interest and dividends received (U.S. Department of the Treasury, 1992a).

In another example, the substitution of a uniform flat-rate consumption tax for domestic capital income taxes would remove distortions in both the location and the magnitude of corporate investment. For example, the "Saving-Exempt Income Tax" proposal of former Senator Sam Nunn and Senator Pete V. Domenici (see the discussion in Seidman, 1997) or the Flat Tax proposal of Robert Hall and Alvin Rabushka (1983, 1995) would replace existing business income taxes with a tax on sales less the cost of purchases from other businesses; in short, domestic investment would be expensed.[45, 46] Because these proposals' intended tax base is consumption, not accrued income as in the current system, they are broadly consistent with a territorial tax system whose design should be considered.

Fundamental tax reform also raises the issue of the effects of required rates of return on debt and equity in capital markets. Replacing the current tax system with the Comprehensive Business Income Tax or the Hall-Rabushka Flat Tax could significantly affect debt and equity returns and international flows of debt and equity capital (see Gentry and Hubbard, 1998). [47]

---

[45]See descriptions in American Business Conference (1993) and Congressional Budget Office (1994). Such a tax is akin to a business transfer tax or substraction-method value-added tax. See for example, former Treasury Secretary Nicholas Brady's (1992) proposal for a business transfer tax.

[46]Alternatively, in the case of a corporate cash flow tax, investment would be expensed and interest deductions would no longer be permitted. In both the saving-exempt income tax and the cash flow tax prototypes, the elimination of interest deductions eliminates the need for interest allocation rules.

[47]The conventional explanation of the effect on interest rates of switching from the current tax system to a broad-based consumption tax such as the Flat Tax is that the pretax interest rate should fall. Consider, for example, the switch from the current tax system to CBIT. Two features of CBIT reform would directly affect corporate interest rates. First, taxes on interest income would be eliminated. Second, interest deductibility would be eliminated. In the simplest story, all interest income is taxed and all interest expenses are deducted. In a closed economy, if there is no heterogeneity in effective tax rates, the introduction of CBIT maintains the existing after-tax interest rate; that is, the pretax interest rate falls by the amount of the tax. In reality, there is heterogeneity in the effective tax rates facing suppliers and demanders of credit. Tax reform could cause downsize capital to flow from currently tax-favored sectors (e.g., housing) to the domestic business sector.

# REFERENCES

Altshuler, R., and P. Fulghieri. 1994. "Incentive effects of foreign tax credits on multinationals." *National Tax Journal* 47:349-361.

Altshuler, R., and J.M. Mintz. 1995. "U.S. interest allocation rules: Effects and policy." *International Taxation and Public Finance* 2:7-35.

Altshuler, R., and T.S. Newlon. 1993. "The effects of U.S. tax policy on the income and repatriation patterns of U.S. multinational corporations." In *Studies in International Taxation,* A. Giovannini, R.G. Hubbard, and J.B. Slemrod, eds. Chicago, Ill.: University of Chicago Press.

Altshuler, R., T.S. Newlon, and W.C. Randolph. 1995. "Tax effects on income repatriation by U.S. multinationals: Evidence from panel data." In *The Effects of Taxation on Multinational Corporations,* M. Feldstein, J.R. Hines, and R.G. Hubbard, eds. Chicago, Ill.: University of Chicago Press.

Alworth, J.S. 1988. *The Finance, Investment and Taxation Decisions of Multinationals.* Oxford: Basil Blackwell.

American Business Conference. 1993. *The Nunn/Domenici Proposal for a Saving-Exempt Income Tax: Overview and Summary.* Conference Pamphlet. Washington, D.C.

Auerbach, A.J., and K.A. Hassett. 1993. "Taxation and foreign direct investment in the United States: A reconstruction of the evidence." In *Studies in International Taxation,* A. Giovannini, R.G. Hubbard, and J.B. Slemrod, eds. Chicago, Ill.: University of Chicago Press.

Ault, H.J., and D.F. Bradford. 1990. "Taxing international income: An analysis of the U.S. system and its economic premises." In *Taxation in the Global Economy,* A. Razin and J.B. Slemrod, eds. Chicago, Ill.: University of Chicago Press.

Blumenthal, M., and J.B. Slemrod. 1994. "The compliance cost of taxing foreign-source income: Its magnitude, determinants, and policy implications." Mimeograph. University of Michigan.

Boskin, M.J., and W.G. Gale. 1987. "New results on the effects of tax policy on the international location of investment." In *The Effects of Taxation on Capital Accumulation,* M. Feldsten, ed. Chicago, Ill.: University of Chicago Press.

Brady, N.F. 1992. Speech to the Graduate School of Business of Columbia University. December 10.

Caves, R.E. 1982. *Multinational Enterprises and Economic Analysis.* Cambridge, Mass.: Cambridge University Press.

Collins, J., and D. Shackleford. 1992. "Foreign tax credit limitations and preferred stock issuances." *Journal of Accounting Research* 30.

Congressional Budget Office. 1994. "Estimates for a prototype saving-exempt income tax." CBO memorandum. Washington, D.C., March.

Cummins, J.G., and R.G. Hubbard. 1995. "The tax sensitivity of foreign direct investment: Evidence from firm-level panel data." In *The Taxation of Multinational Corporations,* M. Feldstein, J.R. Hines, and R.G. Hubbard, eds. Chicago, Ill.: University of Chicago Press.

Cummins, J.G., K.A. Hassett, and R.G. Hubbard. 1994. "A reconsideration of investment behavior using tax reforms as natural experiments." *Brookings Papers on Economic Activity* 2:181-249.

---

In a small open economy, integration increases desired international lending. The effect on interest rates of the shift from CBIT to the Flat Tax depends on the interest sensitivity of the supply of funds to the domestic business sector. If the domestic business sector is a "small open economy," introduction of the Flat Tax leaves interest rates at their CBIT levels. If the supply of funds is not perfectly elastic, the higher demand for funds leads to a decline in the pretax interest rate from its pre-tax reform level by less than the tax wedge.

Fundamental tax reform in the form of the CBIT or Flat Tax would increase the after-tax return on U.S. equities. As a result, fundamental tax reform would likely lead to inflows of equity capital. Such inflows would be attenuated to the extent that domestic capital flows into the domestic business sector as a result of tax reform.

Cummins, J.G., T.S. Harris, and K.A. Hassett. 1995. "Accounting standards, information flow, and firm investment behavior." In *The Taxation of Multinational Corporations,* M. Feldstein, J.R. Hines, and R.G. Hubbard, eds., Chicago, Ill.: University of Chicago Press.

Cummins, J.G., K.A. Hassett, and R.G. Hubbard. 1996. "Tax reforms and investment: A cross-country comparison." *Journal of Public Economics* 62:237-273.

Diamond, P., and J.S. Mirrlees. 1971. "Optimal taxation and public production. I: Production efficiency." *American Economic Review* 61(March):8-27.

Feldstein, M. 1995. "The effects of outbound foreign direct investment on the domestic-capital stock." In *The Taxation of Multinational Corporations,* M. Feldstein, J.R. Hines, and R.G. Hubbard, eds. Chicago, Ill.: University of Chicago Press.

Feldstein, M., J.R. Hines, and R.G. Hubbard, eds. 1995. *The Taxation of Multinational Corporations.* Chicago, Ill.: University of Chicago Press.

French, K.R., and J.M Poterba. 1991. "Investor diversification and international equity markets." *American Economic Review* 81(May):222-226.

Frisch, D.J. 1990. "The economics of international tax policy: Same old and new approaches." *Tax Notes* (April 30).

Froot, K.A., and J.R. Hines, Jr. 1994. "Losing interest: Interest allocation rules and the cost of debt finance." Mimeograph. Harvard University.

Gentry, W.M., and R.G. Hubbard. 1998. "Fundamental tax reform and corporate financial policy." In *Tax Policy and the Economy,* Vol. 12, J. M. Poterba, ed. Cambridge, Mass.: MIT Press.

Gerardi, G., H. Milner, and G. Silverstein. 1994. "The effects of the corporate alternative minimum tax: Additional results from panel data for 1987-1991." *National Tax Association-Tax Institute of America, Proceedings of the 86th Annual Conference,*

Giovannini, A. 1989. "Capital taxation: National tax systems versus the European capital market." *Economic Policy* 4(October).

Giovannini, A., R.G. Hubbard, and J.B. Slemrod, eds. 1993. *Studies in International Taxation.* Chicago, Ill.: University of Chicago Press.

Gordon, R.H., and J. Jun. 1993. "Taxes and the form of ownership of foreign corporate equity." In *Studies in International Taxation,* A. Giovannini, R.G. Hubbard, and J.B. Slemrod, eds. Chicago, Ill: University of Chicago Press.

Gordon, R.H., and J.K. MacKie-Mason. 1995. "Why is there corporate taxation in an open economy? The role of transfer pricing and income shifting." In *The Taxation of Multinational Corporations,* M. Feldstein, J.R. Hines, and R.G. Hubbard, eds. Chicago, Ill.: University of Chicago Press.

Graham, E., and P. Krugman. 1991. *Foreign Direct Investment in the United States.* Washington, D.C.: Institute for International Economics.

Grubert, H., and J. Mutti. 1994. "Taxing multinationals in a world with portfolio flows and R&D: is capital-export neutrality obsolete?" Mimeograph. U.S. Department of the Treasury. Washington, D.C., April.

Hall, B.H. 1993. "The sensitivity of R&D to delicate tax changes: The behavior of U.S. multinationals in the 1980s." Commentary in *Studies in International Taxation,* A. Giovannini, R.G. Hubbard, and J.B. Slemrod, eds. Chicago, Ill.: University of Chicago Press.

Hall, R.E., and A. Rabushka. 1983. *Low Tax, Simple Tax, Flat Tax.* New York: McGraw-Hill.

Hall, R.E., and A. Rabushka. 1995. *The Flat Tax,* 2nd ed. Stanford, Calif.: Hoover Institution Press.

Harris, D., R. Morck, J.B. Slemrod, and B. Yeung. 1993. "Income shifting in U.S. multinational corporations." In *Studies in International Taxation,* A. Giovannini, R.G. Hubbard, and J.B. Slemrod, eds. Chicago, Ill.: University of Chicago Press.

Hartman, D.G. 1984. "Tax policy and foreign direct investment in the United States." *National Tax Journal* 37(December):475-487.

Hartman, D.G. 1985. "Tax policy and fireign direct investment." *Journal of Public Economics* 107-121.

Hines, J.R., Jr., 1993. "On the sensitivity of R&D to delicate tax changes: The behavior of U.S. multinationals in the 1980s." In *Studies in International Taxation*, A. Giovannini, R.G. Hubbard, and J.B. Slemrod, eds. Chicago, Ill.: University of Chicago Press.

Hines, J.R., Jr., and R.G. Hubbard. 1990. "Coming home to America: Dividend repatriation decisions of U.S. multinationals." In *Taxation in the Global Economy*, A. Razin and J.B. Slemrod, eds. Chicago, Ill.: University of Chicago Press.

Hines, J.R., Jr., and E.M. Rice. 1994. "Fiscal paradise: Foreign tax havens and American business. *Quarterly Journal of Economics* 109(February):149-182.

Horst, T. 1980. "A note on the optimal taxation of international investment income." *Quarterly Journal of Economics* 94(June):793-839.

Hufbauer, G.C., assisted by Joanna M. Van Rooij. 1992. *U.S. Taxation of International Income: Blueprint for Reform.* Washington, D.C.: Institute for International Economics.

Hufbauer, G.C., and J.M. Van Rooij. 1994. "U.S. taxation of multinationals: Scoring the Clinton proposals." In *Tax Policy of Economic Growth in the 1990s.* Washington, D.C.: American Council for Capital Formation Center for Policy Research.

Jun, J. 1995. "The impact of international tax rules on the cost of capital." In *The Effects of the Taxation of Multinational Corporations*, M. Feldstein, J.R. Hines, and R.G. Hubbard, eds. Chicago, Ill.: University of Chicago Press.

Jun, J. 1990. "U.S. tax policy and direct investment abroad." In *Taxation in the Global Economy,* A. Razin and J. B. Slemrod, eds. Chicago, Ill.: University of Chicago Press.

Lipsey, R.E. 1995. "Outward direct investment and the U.S. economy." In *The Taxation of Multinational Corporations,* M. Feldstein, J.R. Hines, and R.G. Hubbard, eds. Chicago, Ill.: University of Chicago Press.

Lyon, A.B. 1990. "Investment incentives under the alternative minimum tax." *National Tax Journal* 43:451-465.

Lyon, A.B., and G. Silverstein. 1995. "The alternative minimum tax and the behavior of multinational corporations." In *The Effects of the Taxation of Multinational Corporations*, M. Feldstein, J.R. Hines, and R.G. Hubbard, eds. Chicago, Ill.: University of Chicago Press.

Newlon, T.S. 1987. "Tax policy and the multinational firm's financial policy and investment decisions." Unpublished doctoral dissertation. Princeton University.

Organization for Economic Cooperation and Development. 1991. *Taxing Profits in a Global Economy.* Paris: OECD.

Prakken, J.L. 1994. "Investment, economic growth, and the corporate alternative minimum tax." In *Tax Policy for Economic Growth in the 1990s.* Washington, D.C.: American Council for Capital Formation Center for Policy Research.

Razin, A., and J.B. Slemrod, eds. 1990 *Taxation in a Global Economy.* Chicago, Ill.: University of Chicago Press.

Seidman, L.S. 1997. *The USA Tax: A Progressive Consumption Tax.* Cambridge, Mass.: MIT Press.

Slemrod, J.B. 1990. "Tax effects on foreign direct investment in the United States: Evidence from a cross-country comparison." In *Taxation in a Global Economy,* A. Razin and J.B. Slemrod, eds. Chicago, Ill.: University of Chicago Press.

U.S. Congress. 1990. *Background and Issues Relating to the Taxation of Foreign Investment in the United States.* Washington, D.C.: Joint Committee on Taxation.

U.S. Congress. 1991. *Factors Affecting the International Competitiveness of the United States.* Washington, D.C.: Joint Committee on Taxation.

U.S. Department of the Treasury. 1992a. *Integration of the Individual and Corporate Tax Systems.* Washington, D.C.: U.S. Government Printing Office.

U.S. Department of the Treasury. 1992b. *A Recommendation for Integration of the Individual and Corporate Tax Systems.* Washington, D.C.: U.S. Department of the Treasury.

U.S. Department of the Treasury. 1993. *International Tax Reform: An Interim Report.* Office of Tax Policy. Washington, D.C.: U.S. Department of the Treasury.

U.S. Department of the Treasury. 1997. *Blueprints for Basic Tax Reform.* Washington, D.C.: U.S. Government Printing Office.

# 10

# Directions for International Tax Reform

GARY HUFBAUER
*Institute for International Economics[1]*

This chapter examines the "here and now" of international taxation and prescriptions for the international component of basic tax reform. Between "what is" and what some experts believe "should be," we consider whether countervailing forces will check the pattern in recent years of a stepwise evolution of the international tax system.

## "HERE AND NOW" OF INTERNATIONAL TAXATION

In the 1950s, 1960s, and even the 1970s, the United States entertained a "grand vision" of the international tax system. This vision was built around several foundation facts and assumptions (Hufbauer, 1992):
Countries that were important players in the international economy generally operated "classical" tax systems, consisting of separate corporate and individual income taxes. It was thought that these systems could be satisfactorily meshed, on a bilateral basis, through a series of tax treaties.

- Sales, excise, value-added, and kindred consumption taxes were put in a separate conceptual box. Their international aspects—namely, the extent that they could be adjusted at the border—were addressed in the General Agreement on Tariffs and Trade (GATT), which has now become the World Trade Organization (WTO).
- Most business and personal income was tightly "linked" to one nation or another and not easily shifted as a way of avoiding taxes. Most interna-

---

[1]The views in this chapter are the opinions of the author and do not necessarily reflect the opinions of the institute, its board of trustees, or its advisory board.

tional firms were structured in a hierarchical parent-subsidiary relationship relationship, with capital flowing from the parent to the subsidiary and income flowing in the other direction. Most individuals who earned income abroad did so in the form of wages and salaries.

- The network of purchases and sales of goods and services between related corporate taxpayers was not dense. Most of these transactions could be compared with similar transactions between unrelated parties to determine a fair "arm's-length" price so that income and expense could not be shifted between jurisdictions for the purpose of tax avoidance.

In this world, the key tasks of international tax officials, acting as revenue collectors, were to determine the "source" of income and the "residence" of the taxpayer. "Source rules" evolved naturally from the links between geography and income. "Residence rules" were built on the place of business organization or the place where the individual spent most of his working time.

Once source and residence rules were agreed between countries, it was a matter of dickering to establish which country, the source country or the residence country, had the primary right to tax the income in question and which had the secondary right. Most of the dickering was done in bilateral tax treaties. The source country was generally assigned primary taxation rights to the particular stream of income. This primary right was recognized by the residence country when it exempted the income from its own tax net or when it allowed a credit against its own taxes for foreign taxes paid on the income (the foreign tax credit). Within the treaty framework, however, source countries usually agreed to cap particular taxes (e.g., a 10 percent limit on withholding taxes imposed on royalty income).

Up to this point, the conceptual framework had little economic rationale, except to avoid "double taxation." Double taxation was regarded as a vice, based on the argument that it would discourage international trade and investment.

The United States contributed two economic doctrines to the system. The most important was "capital export neutrality." The principle, inconsistently applied, was that U.S. firms and residents should not have a tax incentive to operate outside the United States. Latent tax inducements would be offset by the U.S. system of taxing worldwide income; any U.S. firm or resident would eventually pay the same overall rate of tax, no matter where in the world it operated. This would be achieved by taxing the worldwide income of U.S. firms and residents and allowing a credit for foreign taxes imposed on foreign-source income. As the principal home country for multinational corporations and a country with relatively high corporate tax rates in the 1950s and 1960s, the United States provided an "umbrella" that invited other countries to raise their corporate rates to the U.S. level.

The second economic doctrine was that foreign countries should not practice tax discrimination against U.S. firms. Taken together, nondistortion and nondiscrimination constituted the original "level playing field": U.S. firms should, in the long run, not pay less tax when operating abroad than when operating at home and foreign governments should not tax U.S. firms more heavily than they taxed their own or third-country firms. Like all level playing field concepts, this was laden with inconsistencies that became more apparent over time.

By the 1980s, many events had converged to erode these foundation facts and assumptions about the workings of the international economy and the proper role of the international tax system. For one thing, many industrial countries abandoned their "classical" systems of income taxation for "integrated" systems that gave recognition at the personal level for taxes paid at the corporate level. The proper way to "mesh" classical and integrated systems across international boundaries is not at all obvious.

Second, many industrial countries placed more emphasis on the role of sales, excise, value-added, and other consumption taxes in their fiscal structures. These taxes have important consequences that are unevenly addressed by the rules of GATT and the WTO (Hufbauer, 1996). Moreover, the doctrine of capital export neutrality cannot be implemented satisfactorily without taking these other taxes and production subsidies into account.

New forms of international income and expense exploded-technology income of various types from movie royalties to patent licensing fees; plain vanilla-and-chocolate sundae portfolio income (interest and dividends and gains and losses from dealing in foreign exchange and derivatives); electronic commerce (both telecommunications transmission services and various sorts of remote value-added services); business, artistic, and professional services (Bechtel to Michael Jackson to Arthur Andersen); and huge intracorporate sales of goods and services. Source and residence rules are not obvious for many of these new forms of income and types of expenses. In many cases, comparable transactions between unrelated taxpayers do not exist or are highly idiosyncratic, so there are few ready benchmarks for applying the arm's-length pricing standard.

The combination of global integration, new forms of income and expense, and increasing sophistication among corporate taxpayers loosened the old links between geography and income. Increasingly, firms learned to "game" the tax systems of the world, not only to alter source and residence on paper but also to change the location of plants, R&D facilities, and headquarters operations.

Between the 1960s and 1980s, the United States relative to other industrial nations exchanged its position as the country with high personal and corporate marginal tax rates for a new position as a low income tax country. Since the mid-1980s, however, the United States has once again drifted up into the high corporate tax ranks, as established industrial countries and emerging industrial powers have cut their own corporate rates. At the same time, multinational corporations based in Europe, Asia, and Latin America have come to play a much larger role in the world economy. These developments meant that U.S. leverage as a disciplinarian of tax distortions and tax discrimination diminished and Treasury Department revenues from U.S. firms' operations abroad shrank relative to revenues from foreign firms doing business in the United States.

What has been the U.S. response to the altered landscape of the global economy? Senator Russell Long (D-LA) said it all in his famous aphorism, "Don't tax you, don't tax me, tax the fellow behind the tree!" U.S. and foreign multinationals are the quintessential "fellow behind the tree"—big, rich, and cavalier in the eyes of tax populists.

The Tax Reform Act of 1986 marked the turning point. The conceptual foundations of U.S. international tax policy, already eroded by global forces, were all but ignored in the search for revenue. In this search, the guiding light had been created years earlier by Stanley S. Surrey, a distinguished professor at the Harvard Law School and Assistant Secretary for Tax Policy during the Kennedy and Johnson administrations. Surrey's searchlight was his list of "tax expenditures," a schedule of revenue lost by departures from an "ideal" tax system. Surrey's ideal basically amounted to a flat-rate, broad-base, classical tax system.

This ideal is too simplistic for the realities of international taxation. It ignores the fact that whereas the U.S. Congress can, if it wishes, establish uniform taxation across all states and sectors of the U.S. economy, it has no such power for the rest of the world. In a global economy where the United States is one among several important players, the realities of competition must be taken into account. The tax expenditure concept ignores this fundamental fact.

Despite this basic flaw, Surrey's ideal tax system has long been used to generate the Treasury Department's tax expenditure estimates. These numbers were picked up by congressional tax staff, were suitably polished, and became objects of desire in the 1986 tax reform debate. Basically, revenue goals were pushed wherever there was a soft spot in the collective armory of multinational firms, and wherever foreign retaliation would not be too severe. The result is a great deal more complexity and somewhat more revenue (Hufbauer, 1992).

Much the same process has continued to dominate international tax legislation since the Tax Reform Act of 1986. Indeed, as McClure and Ossi (1997) point out, despite widespread recognition that U.S. taxation of international income has become mindlessly complex, and despite many proposals for simplifying the system and giving it direction, only one small reform has been enacted since 1986—the repeal of Internal Revenue Code section 956A.

The year 1997 saw a modest revival of tax populism of the 1986 vintage. The difference between 1997 and 1986 is that the term "tax expenditures" is too dry and technical for present needs; it has been replaced by the more emotive term "corporate welfare." Missing from both the 1986 drive to reduce tax expenditures and the current drive to curtail corporate welfare is any coherent articulation of the purposes of the tax system in shaping the U.S. role in the international economy.

Instead, the tax writers simply turn to the tax expenditures schedule and

**TABLE 10.1**   Office of Management and Budget 1996 Estimates of Potential Revenue from Eliminating Selected Tax Expenditures (billions of dollars)

|  | 1997 | 1997-2001 |
| --- | --- | --- |
| Exclusion of income of foreign sales corporations | 1.6 | 9.0 |
| Inventory property sales source rule expections (the export source rule) | 1.5 | 8.5 |
| Interest allocation rules exception for certain financial operations | 0.1 | 0.4 |
| Deferral of income from controlled foreign corporations | 2.0 | 12.1 |

search for opportunities to raise revenue. What was on the list? The fiscal year 1997 budget listed the corporate tax expenditure items shown in Table 10.1, with figures for both 1997 and the five years 1997-2001.

In 1997, there was an assault on the export source rule and modest attempts to curb deferral. Some members of Congress pushed to replace the arm's-length pricing standard by a formula approach. None of these proposed changes made any headway. Abroad, some countries would like to tax payments for electronic commerce (e.g., payments for seismic analysis done in the United States for drilling operations conducted in the South China Sea). However, new "source" taxes on electronic commerce were strongly resisted by the U.S. Department of the Treasury (1996).

## COUNTERVAILING FORCES

What countervailing forces could alter the evolution of the international tax system, which is now decisively shaped by revenue considerations? In my judgment, four forces are working in a more positive direction. To a certain extent, they were evident in the 1997 debate.

First, many countries have come to see multinational corporations as an ally, not an enemy. The degree of affection differs from country to country and sector to sector. In situations where local, especially state-owned, enterprises have a major presence and in situations such as natural resources and basic telecommunications where economic rents are abundant, the welcome mat may not be fully extended. However, over the past 20 years, more countries have come to see the advantages of an active presence of foreign corporations in more sectors of the domestic economy (Graham, 1996a). This trend is almost sure to continue. As it proceeds, more countries will adapt their tax systems to attract firms, especially high-technology firms, corporate headquarters, and R&D facilities.

Among countries of the Organization for Economic Cooperation and Development (OECD), for example, Spain, Canada, and Australia have the most attractive R&D packages for large firms, whereas Germany, Italy, and New Zealand have the least generous packages (OECD, 1996). In the next decade, countries such as Brazil, Argentina, Chile, Singapore, China, and India are likely to become important competitors for high-tech firms and R&D facilities. Currently, the United States is "king of the mountain" among industrial countries in terms of R&D effort, corporate vitality, and economic growth. To keep this position, the United States will have to adapt its tax system to remain at least as hospitable as its major competitors.

The second countervailing force is growing recognition of the economic gains associated with larger exports of goods and services. Export growth has contributed about 28 percent of real U.S. gross domestic product (GDP) expansion in the past four years, even though exports in 1992 accounted for only 10 percent of the U.S. economy. More important, studies by Richardson and Rindal (1996) and the U.S. Department of Commerce (1996) demonstrate that export jobs pay a wage and salary premium of about 15 percent more than comparable jobs in other sectors of the economy. These facts, energetically advertised by the Clinton administration (Magaziner, 1996), are gaining acceptance among the American public. Within a few years, tax measures that harm U.S. export capabilities may be regarded with the same disapproval that would be visited on tax measures that discourage education or R&D.

The third countervailing force is the demonstrably strong connection, at least for the United States, between foreign direct investment (FDI) and U.S. exports. Research to which I contributed a few years ago shows that U.S. exports to a given country rise by about 2.5 percent for every 10 percent increase in U.S. direct investment in that country (Hufbauer et al., 1994). Graham (1996b) also finds a strong positive correlation between U.S. foreign direct investment and U.S. exports after allowing for the normal "gravity model" variables—income per capita, population, and distance.

Increasingly, foreign direct investment is an essential component of corporate export efforts. This is especially true for high-technology customized goods and services that require hands-on interaction between seller and buyer and extensive after-sale maintenance. One reason the United States exports so little to Japan, Korea, and China is that local policies in these countries have long kept U.S. multinationals at bay. These policies are being transformed for reasons already discussed. To expand its export position in Asia and elsewhere, the United States will have to do its part by maintaining a competitive tax climate for U.S. firms that invest abroad.

The fourth countervailing force is the responsiveness of production location decisions to corporate tax rates, documented in a recent report for the Export Source Coalition (Hufbauer and DeRosa, 1997). Although "older" studies (dating from 1981) surveyed by Hines (1996a) cannot be summarized by a single number, a rough characterization of their results is that a 1 percentage point increase in the effective business tax rate induces a 1 percent decrease in the stock of plant and equipment—in other words an elasticity coefficient of 1.0.

However, recent scholarship has detected significantly larger effects. Grubert and Mutti (1996) estimated an elasticity coefficient of 3.0 for U.S. foreign direct investment placed in various locations. In another paper, Hines (1996b) esti-mated that a 1 percentage point increase in a state's corporate tax rate (e.g., from 6 to 7 percent) would reduce inward foreign investment in the state by about 10 percent. Finally, in a paper studying the effect of taxation and corruption on direct investment flows from 14 "home" countries to 34 "host" countries, Wei (1997) estimated an elasticity coefficient of 5.0 for the impact of the host country's tax rate.

Recent scholarship uses more sophisticated econometric techniques than the earlier work surveyed by Hines, but there is more to the story than an improved ability to detect production response rates. With the integration of the world economy and the sharp decline of major political risks—communism, socialism, expropriation, and protectionism—firms have in all liklihood become more re-sponsive to differential tax rates. The consequences of high response rates can be dramatic. Hufbauer and DeRosa (1997) calculate, for example, that repealing the export source rule, a leading target on the administration's 1997 tax agenda, could ultimately reduce U.S. exports by about $33.5 billion (in the year 2000) as firms relocate production abroad and knock about $1.9 billion off the wage and salary premiums associated with high-paying export jobs—for a revenue gain of only $1.6 billion. Similar adverse consequences might result from eliminating the foreign sales corporation or repealing the deferral provisions of U.S. tax law.

To summarize, it seems likely that a chain of competitive consequences— running from friendly tax climates abroad, to wage and salary premiums in U.S. export industries, to the link between U.S. foreign direct investment and U.S. exports, to the production response of export activities to tax differentials—are beginning to shift the current focus on revenue collection as the touchstone of U.S. tax policy, making a sensible international component of basic tax reform easier to implement.

## INTERNATIONAL COMPONENT OF BASIC TAX REFORM

The fundamental goals of basic tax reform, along the lines of the flat tax or the Nunn-Domenici USA (unlimited savings allowance) tax, are to promote sav-ings and investment and to simplify the tax system. There is little reason to endorse the upheaval and agony of basic tax reform unless you believe three things: (1) savings and investment will rise significantly in response to a con-sumption-oriented tax system (Hubbard and Skinner 1996); (2) higher savings and investment will augment the long-term rate of U.S. GDP growth from, say, 2.5 to 3.5 percent; and (3) tax simplification is very desirable, even if some people pay more taxes. In the overall scheme of things, the international aspects of basic tax reform are secondary to these fundamental goals.

That said, the international consequences would be significant. The design of basic tax reform proposals is essentially "territorial." Corporate income earned within the United States would be subject to U.S. tax; corporate income earned abroad would not. This basic change would ensure that U.S. firms operating abroad could compete on the same tax terms as foreign firms. On balance, this feature would not cost revenue because foreign subsidiaries operating in the United States could no longer deduct interest payments to their overseas parent corporations. The additional revenue collected on the U.S. operations of foreign subsidiaries would make up for any tax revenue lost on the overseas operations of U.S. subsidiaries.

Once the territorial aspect of the reformed tax system is understood and accepted, it leaves an important international question: What is the proper tax treatment of exports and imports of goods and services? I have analyzed the economic and legal aspects of this question elsewhere (Hufbauer, 1996). Here, I sketch the central issues that are likely to arise when the debate is joined. For brevity, they are stated as political and economic propositions.

The first political proposition is that imported goods and services should be taxed the same as domestically produced goods and services. This will guard against an apparent tax incentive to produce abroad and sell the goods and services back into the U.S. market. Exceptions to symmetrical tax treatment between imports and domestic production should be negotiated country by country or with regional groups such as the European Union on a reciprocal basis.

The second political proposition is that business profits earned on U.S. export sales should be treated the same as business profits earned on production abroad. In other words, these profits should be excluded from the U.S. tax net. Otherwise there will be an apparent incentive to locate abroad rather than produce in the United States for the export market.

In addition to these political propositions about basic tax reform, some less evident economic propostions should be taken into account. There are two basic principles for making adjustments at the border for domestic taxation-the destination principle and the origin principle. Under the destination principle, domestic taxes are imposed on imports of goods and services but not on exports. Under the origin principle, the reverse happens: domestic taxes are not imposed on imports, but they are on exports.

In theory, exchange rate changes can offset border tax adjustments, both in terms of the overall U.S. trade balance position and in terms of the relative attractiveness of the United States as a place to invest. However, the impact of exchange rate changes will almost certainly differ, sector by sector, from the impact of border tax adjustments. Moreover, not one person in 10 understands the macroeconomic equivalence between exchange rate changes and border tax adjustments. These are two powerful reasons for endorsing the destination principle.

The impact of basic tax reform on the domestic savings-investment balance will be the primary determinant of the trade balance consequences of tax reform. The presence or absence of border tax adjustments and changes in the U.S. system of taxing foreign income are secondary considerations. If basic tax reform increases U.S. savings more than it increases U.S. investment, the U.S. trade balance will "improve." If tax reform increases U.S. investment more than savings, the trade balance will "worsen." That said, the success of basic tax reform will be judged far more by its investment consequences than by its trade balance consequences. The destination principle is more friendly to investment than the origin principle since it automatically creates tax parity between domestic production both in competition with imports and in export markets. Destination principle adjustments require more administrative machinery, however, and create a new form of tax on international transactions. This is particularly troublesome for rapidly growing electronic commerce. Destination principle adjustments would require, for example, U.S. taxation of data analysis in Singapore performed for a U.S. bank or payments by U.S. firms to France Telecom for the transmission of voice, data, or video signals.

From these political and economic considerations, I draw a few major conclusions about the international aspects of basic tax reform. First, destination principle border adjustments should be part of basic tax reform legislation. The President should be authorized, however, to negotiate origin principle taxation on a reciprocal basis, sector by sector, country by country. A system of origin principle taxation might be negotiated with Canada and Mexico, and globally for electronic commerce, before European and other countries attach value-added taxes to electronic purchases.

Presumably, origin principle taxation would be negotiated only with countries and in sectors that implement business tax systems similar to the reformed U.S. system. Origin principle taxation would apply equally to value-added, sales and corporate income taxes; otherwise, U.S. firms would still be paying value added taxes on their exports to Europe and elsewhere. Also, the origin principle would be negotiated only in contexts where the United States is reasonably assured that it would not lead to tax avoidance, for example, transshipment of French goods through Canada and then to the United States to avoid U.S. border tax adjustments on direct imports from France. The similarity of tax systems, comprehensive character of the origin principle where negotiated, and the antiabuse provisions would guard against tax incentives for production relocation.

Under the origin principle, the United States would not collect revenue on imports of goods and services but would collect revenue on exports of goods and services. Because bilateral trade would seldom be balanced, one country or the other would collect more revenue from application of the origin principle rather than the destination principle. In some contexts, supplementary provisions might be negotiated between the partners to achieve some degree of revenue equalization. As a normal matter, however, adoption of the origin principle would amount to acceptance of the implied division of revenue.

## REFERENCES

Graham, E.M. 1996a. *Global Corporations and National Governments.* Washington, D.C. Institute for International Economics.

Graham, E.M. 1996b. "The relationships between trade and foreign direct investment in the manufacturing sector: Empirical results for the United States and Japan." In *Does Ownership Matter: Japanese Multinationals in East Asia,* D. Encarnation, ed. London: Oxford University Press.

Grubert, H., and J. Mutti. 1996. "Do taxes influence where U.S. corporations invest?" Paper prepared for the Conference on Trans-Atlantic Public Economics Seminar, Amsterdam, May 29-31 (revised August 1996; available from Grubert at the U.S Treasury Department).

Hines, J.R. 1996a. "Tax Policy and the Activities of Multinational Corporations." Working Paper 5589. National Bureau of Economic Research, Cambridge, Mass., May.

Hines, J.R. 1996b. "Altered states: Taxes and the location of foreign direct investment in America." *American Economic Review* 85(5).

Hubbard, R.G., and J.S. Skinner. 1996. "Assessing the effectiveness of savings incentives." *Journal of Economic Perspectives* 10(4).

Hufbauer, G.C., assisted by J. van Rooij. 1992. *U.S. Taxation of International Income*, Washington D.C.: Institute for International Economics.

Hufbauer, G.C., assisted by C. Gabyzon. 1996. *Fundamental Tax Reform and Border Tax Adjustments.* Washington D.C.: Institute for International Economics.

Hufbauer, G.C. and D.A. DeRosa. 1997. "Costs and Benefits of the Export Source Rule." *Tax Notes International* 14(20).

Hufbauer, G.C., D. Lakdawalla, and A. Malani. 1994. "Determinants of direct foreign investment and its connection to trade." *UNCTAD Review.*

Magaziner, I. 1996. "An interview with Ira Magaziner." *The International Economy* X(6).

McClure, W.P., and G.J. Ossi. 1997. "Legislative proposals to reform and simplify the U.S. taxation of foreign income." *Tax Notes International* 14(5).

Office of Management and Budget. 1996. *Budget of the United States Government. Analytical Perspectives. Fiscal Year 1997.* Washington D.C.: Office of Management and Budget.

Organization for Economic Cooperation and Development. 1996. *Fiscal Measures to Promote R&D and Innovation.* Directorate for Science, Technology and Industry. Paris: OECD.

Richardson, J.D., and K. Rindal. 1996. *Why Exports Matter: More!* Washington, D.C.: Institute for International Economics and the Manufacturing Institute.

U.S. Department of Commerce. 1996. *U.S. Jobs Supported by Exports of Goods and Services.* Washington D.C.: Economics and Statistics Administration.

U.S. Department of the Treasury. 1996. *Selected Tax Policy Implications of Global Electronic Commerce.* Washington, D.C.: Office of Tax Policy.

Wei, S. 1997. How Taxing Is Corruption on International Behavior? Kennedy School of Government. Cambridge Mass.: Harvard University

# 11

# Tax Reform:
# Prescriptions and Prospects

THOMAS A. BARTHOLD[1]
*Joint Committee on Taxation, U.S. Congress*

The chapters by Glenn Hubbard and Peter Merrill very ably describe how fundamental tax reform might affect businesses that engage in cross-border sales, production, and research. My comments are confined to three areas. First, what does economic analysis tell us about the policy question of whether and to what extent the research and development expenditures of these businesses should be subsidized? Second, what is the tax treatment of R&D under current tax reform proposals? Third, what are the prospects for fundamental tax reform?

There are two strands of academic research that investigate the research activities and investment decisions of multinational enterprises. The first strand comes from scholars in the field of industrial organization and is typified by the work of Caves (1982). This strand analyzes the multinational firm as possessing substantial holdings of intangible capital, brand names, patents, know-how, and the like. The research emphasizes that to exploit its intangible capital more fully the firm may have to locate overseas as well as in the United States. Because physical capital is complementary to intangible capital, exploitation of intangible assets may motivate investment abroad by U.S.-based multinationals. Likewise, with a physical presence overseas, the multinational may find it profitable to develop additional intangible assets overseas by undertaking R&D. This strand of research generally ignores tax policy as a factor in the overseas location of intangible and physical capital. It emphasizes that there are economically valid reasons to invest abroad and to engage in R&D abroad. Peter Nugent's observations about the market's dictating Merck's overseas presence is a concrete illustration of this strand of academic research.

---

[1]These comments are the author's alone and should not be construed to reflect the views of any member of the United States Congress or of the staff of the Joint Committee on Taxation.

The second body of research comes from scholars in the field of public finance. The work of Hines (1993) and his chapter in this volume typify this analysis of the research activities and investment decisions of multinational enterprises. Here the emphasis is squarely on the extent to which taxes matter to the decision to invest abroad or undertake research abroad relative to undertaking the same activities in the United States. With apologies to Hines's more sophisticated econometrics, one can think of the empirical work of the public finance economists as estimating an equation of the following sort.

$$R = \alpha + \beta (1 - t), \tag{1}$$

where R is research expenditures and $(1 - t)$ is the classic public finance characterization of the "tax price" of an activity. Hines finds statistically significant and quantitatively large bs. That is, the tax price matters to the research decisions of multinational enterprises.

Unfortunately, there has been no synthesis of these two strands of literature. The industrial organization economist pays scant attention to taxes as a factor in the multinational's decisions. Similarly, public finance economists pay scant attention to factors beyond taxes. In terms of equation (1), above, the work of industrial organization economists is about explaining the a term, whereas the work of public finance economists is about explaining the b term.

Lack of a synthesis makes it difficult to answer the overriding policy question: Does society in general and do U.S.-based multinationals in particular undertake the "right" amount of R&D? Because of spillover effects (positive externalities) from the creation of knowledge, a case can be made for subsidizing R&D and for worrying where the spillover occurs.[2] However, economists have not identified what the "right" amount of R&D is. Equation (1) can help us think about this policy question. It says that some R&D activities are going to occur despite the use of policy tools; that is, some R&D activities are inframarginal. The a term can be thought of as the inframarginal component. Equation (1) also states that R&D responds at the margin to tax policy changes. If the inframarginal component is large, and large in comparison to the marginal component, there may be less concern about the effect of the tax price than if the inframarginal component is small. Without a synthesis of the academic research it is difficult to assess whether or to what extent R&D should be subsidized and the efficacy of tax policy as a tool to be used to increase social welfare.

My second comment amplifies the contributions of Hubbard and Merrill with respect to how consumption-based tax reform proposals treat R&D expenditures—and more generally all expenditures that create intangible assets—compared to the treatment of these expenditures under the current income tax. The key point is that a consumption tax puts investment in physical capital on a par

---

[2]The literature does not adequately address a second policy question: If R&D is subsidized to account for the positive externalities of knowledge creation, does it matter whether the R&D occurs in the United States or abroad?

with investment in intangible capital—all such investments are expensed. Under the income tax system, investments in intangible capital generally are expensed whereas investments in physical capital generally are depreciated. In addition, certain R&D expenditures qualify for a further credit. Replacement of the income tax with a consumption tax is unquestionably good for investment in physical capital. The effect on intangible capital is ambiguous. Investment in physical capital is advantaged relative to investment in intangible capital. Because of complementarities between physical and intangible investment, if aggregate investment increases, intangible capital may benefit. Also, as the Joint Committee on Taxation (JCT) staff described in a recent report (JCT, 1996), a consumption tax may encourage the location of intangible capital in the United States rather than abroad. The big policy question remains unanswered. Is the amount of R&D that would be undertaken under a consumption tax the socially optimal amount; that is, does it account for the positive externalities?

Many people ask, "Is fundamental tax reform on the table?" I think it is fair to say that fundamental tax reform is not on the table, but perhaps it is in the kitchen. There is strong interest in fundamental reform in Congress. One need only examine the names of people associated with the topic to conclude that tax reform—if not "on the table"—is "in the kitchen": Bill Archer, Chairman of the House Ways and Means Committee; Dick Armey, Majority Leader of the House of Representatives; Pete Domenici, Chairman of the Senate Budget Committee; and in the past Bill Roth, Chairman of the Finance Committee, have all expressed interest in fundamental reform.

That said, in the short run, further piecemeal reform affecting the income taxation of U.S.-based multinationals is more likely. As an example, the last Congress passed a repeal of Internal Revenue Code section 956A. The President has proposed, and Congress recently enacted, reform of the foreign sales corporation rules relating to software sales abroad. Two bills in the 104th Congress, S. 2086 introduced by then-Senator Larry Pressler and H.R. 1690 introduced by Representative Amo Houghton, included provisions for treating all operations in any European Union country as being from one country and eliminating overlapping taxation under rules relating to passive foreign investment companies and rules relating to controlled foreign corporations. This latter provision was included in the recently enacted Taxpayer Relief Act of 1997. I would expect interest in smaller-scale reform of this sort within the current income tax to continue in the 105th Congress.

## REFERENCES

Caves, Richard E. 1982. *Multinational Enterprises and Economic Analysis.* Cambridge, Mass.: Cambridge University Press.

Hines, James R., Jr. 1993. "On the sensitivity of R&D to delicate tax changes: The behavior of U.S. multinationals in the 1980s." In *Studies in International Taxation*, A. Giovannini, R.G. Hubbard, and J.B. Slemrod, eds. Chicago, Ill.: University of Chicago Press.

Joint Committee on Taxation. 1996. *Impact on International Competitiveness of Replacing the Federal Income Tax* (JCS-5-96). Washington, D.C.

# Glossary

**Active income:**  Although not a statutory or regulatory term it is generally understood as income generated from the active conduct of a trade or business
(e.g., making widgets).  Technically, it is the residual left after passive and
other types of income defined by statute or regulation have been identified.
[Cf. Passive income.]

**Alternative incremental research and experimentation credit**:  An alternative
method a taxpayer may elect to use in calculating the research and experimentation tax credit, based on comparing certain percentages of qualified
research expense to certain percentages of average annual gross receipts.
[Cf. Research and experimentation credit.]

**Alternative minimum tax (corporate)**:  An alternative tax typically imposed on
firms with low taxable income as calculated under the regular corporate income tax.  The tax rate is generally 20 percent rather than 35 percent but
applied to a broader income base than the regular corporate income tax because certain deductions, credits, and allowances permitted under the regular
tax are added back to income for AMT purposes.

**Capital export neutrality**:  The principle that the tax system should not provide
incentives for U.S. firms and residents to operate outside the United States
by taxing domestic income more heavily than foreign income.

**Capital import neutrality**:  The principle that the income from all investments
within a country should face the same tax burden, regardless of the nationality of the investor.

**Comprehensive Business Income Tax (CBIT)**:  A proposal advanced by the
U.S. Treasury Department in 1992 that would integrate the corporate and
personal income taxes so that corporate-source income would be taxed only

once, rather than twice, as under the current system. CBIT would effectively make the corporation tax a withholding tax on corporate source income.

**Deferral:** The general rule that the foreign earnings of foreign corporations are not taxable in the United States currently even though the foreign corporation is controlled by a U.S. shareholder or shareholders, usually a U.S. multinational parent corporation. Such earnings arc taxable in the United States when paid to the U.S. shareholder, usually as dividends, interest, or royalties.

**Destination principle taxation**: A hypothetical system in which a country taxes imports of goods and services but not exports. [Cf. Origin principle taxation.]

**Excess limitation**: The position of a U.S. corporation when the average foreign tax rate on its foreign-source income is less than the average U.S. tax on the same foreign-source income. This phrase derives from the fact that foreign tax credits generally are limited to an amount equal to the U.S. tax rate multiplied by a taxpayer's foreign source income. When a taxpayer is not affected by this limitation, it has limitation remaining or "excess limitation." [Cf. Foreign tax credit.]

**Export source rule**: A tax code provision (section 863(b)) that permits firms to claim that half of the profits on any sale which "passes title" in a foreign country were generated abroad.

**Flat tax**: A broad class of proposals to broaden the tax base and lower marginal tax rates, generally to a single marginal tax rate. In the Hall-Rabushka flat tax proposal, individuals and firms would be taxed at the same rate, and individuals would be taxed only on their wages, benefits, and pension payouts. Capital income would not be part of the tax base, so the flat tax would be a consumption tax.

**Foreign sales corporation rules**: A set of tax provisions, introduced in 1984 as a replacement for DISC (Domestic International Sales Corporations), that allows some tax deferral on U.S. export profits, when the taxpayer employs a "foreign sales corporation" as defined by the Internal Revenue Code.

**Foreign tax credit:** To avoid double taxation of the same income, U.S-based multinational companies may claim a credit against U.S. tax liabilities for taxes paid to foreign jurisdictions on income earned within those foreign jurisdictions. [Cf. Foreign tax credit limitations and excess limitation.]

**Foreign tax credit limitation:** To avoid the claiming of foreign tax credits against domestic U.S. income, the United States limits foreign tax credits generally to either lower taxes paid to foreign jurisdictions or an amount equal to the U.S. tax rate multiplied by the taxpayer's foreign source income. When a taxpayer has paid taxes abroad at a rate higher than the U.S. rate, such that it may not claim credit for all of its foreign taxes because of the foreign tax credit limitation, the taxpayer is said to be in an "excess credit" position. [Cf. Foreign tax credit, excess limitation, and section 904(d).]

**General Agreement on Tariffs and Trade (GATT):** The umbrella multilateral trade agreement addressing tariffs and non-tariff barriers and providing means of resolving disputes. [Cf. World Trade Organization.]

**Interest allocation rules:** Rules issued under Section 1.861-8 that specify the portion of interest expenses incurred in the United States that multinational firms must charge against foreign-source income for purposes of calculating their foreign tax credit limitation. [Cf. Foreign tax credit limitation.]

**National Retail Sales Tax:** A form of national consumption tax, sometimes proposed as an alternative to the current U.S. income tax, which would use a point-of-sale retail sales tax to raise revenue.

**Origin principle taxation:** A hypothetical system in which a country taxes exports of goods and services but not imports of goods and services. [Cf. Destination principle taxation.]

**Passive foreign investment company (PFIC):** Any foreign corporation with excessive passive income (75 percent or more) or excessive passive assets (50 percent or more) is a PFIC. A U.S. shareholder of a PFIC generally must either forego deferral on the PFIC's income and subject that income to current U.S. taxation, even if not distributed to that shareholder, or defer taxation until the income is distributed but pay interest based on the deferral period. [Cf. Deferral and subpart F.]

**Passive income:** Investment income such as interest or dividends not generated from the active conduct of a trade or business. Passive income is generally not bound by geography. For example, a U.S. taxpayer can earn interest in the United States by depositing excess cash in a U.S. bank or abroad by depositing cash in a foreign bank. [Cf. Active income.]

**Research and experimentation credit:** Currently, a 20 percent credit for the amount by which a corporate taxpayer's qualified research expenditures (primarily for wages and supplies) for a tax year exceed a base amount. First instituted in 1981, the credit has been modified and extended several times, most recently in the 1997 tax bill. [Cf. Alternative research and experimentation credit.]

**Residence basis:** A national tax system, such as that of the United States, in which resident individuals and corporations are taxed on income earned abroad as well as domestically. In such countries, double taxation is avoided typically by granting a credit for taxes paid to the foreign jurisdiction in which the income is earned, which is considered to be the "primary" taxing jurisdiction. [Cf. Foreign tax credit and territorial basis.]

**Section 1.861-8 allocation rules:** U.S. Treasury regulations governing U.S. multinational corporations' allocation of U.S. expenses, such as interest and R&D, between domestic and foreign-source income for purposes of calculating the foreign tax credit limitation. The 861-8 rules as they apply to R&D were first issued in 1977 and have been modified by statute and regulation several times since.

**Section 174:** The general rule that companies may deduct 100 percent of qualifying research and development expenses in the year incurred rather than capitalizing such expenses and depreciating them over a number of years.

**Section 904(d):** The section of the Internal Revenue Code that creates separate foreign tax credit limitations for separate categories or "baskets" of income, such as active income, passive income, financial services income, and several other categories of income.

**Section 904(g):** The section of the Internal Revenue Code that treats certain income earned by foreign subsidiaries as domestic rather than foreign source, to curtail the parent company's ability to absorb foreign tax credits.

**Section 956A:** A section of the Internal Revenue Code (enacted in 1993 and repealed in 1996) that was designed to prevent the build-up of excessive cash and other passive assets in controlled foreign subsidiaries by imposing current U.S. taxation (i.e., eliminating deferral) once a certain threshold of passive assets was reached.

**Subpart F anti-deferral provisions:** Rules enacted in 1962 and subsequently modified to impose current U.S. taxation (i.e., eliminate deferral) on foreign-source income by treating certain income, generally income between related parties or passive income, as if it had been distributed currently to the U.S. parent company, thereby subjecting it to current tax. These rules generally apply to foreign corporations at least 50 percent owned by U.S. persons holding stakes of at least 10 percent each.

**10-50 Ventures:** Joint ventures between U.S. and foreign firms in which the U.S. firm owns between a 10 and 50 percent stake. Foreign tax credits from such ventures are calculated separately from the credits associated with other foreign earnings of the U.S. firm, so that the credits cannot be "averaged" together. [Cf. Section 904(d).]

**Territorial basis:** A national tax system in which resident individuals and corporations are taxed only on income earned within the country's borders. In such a system, foreign tax credits are not necessary to avoid double taxation on income earned in a foreign jurisdiction. [Cf. Residence basis.]

**USA (Unlimited Savings Allowance) Tax:** A form of national consumption tax proposed by Senators Sam Nunn and Pete Domenici to replace the current U.S. income tax system. The USA tax would expand current IRA-type arrangements to permit individuals to deduct their net savings from their taxable income. In conjunction with corporate income tax changes this would effectively exclude corporate and other capital income from the tax base.

**World Trade Organization (WTO):** The international institution established by the parties to the GATT in 1995 for negotiating trade agreements and resolving trade disputes. [Cf. General Agreement on Tariffs and Trade.]

# Index

flat-rate consumption tax, 127
flat tax, 84
foreign-source earnings, 7
foreign tax credit, 100–101
impact on business decision making, 5–6
implications for capital markets, 127
incremental, 100, 104
interest allocation rules, 125, 126
international context, 87, 139–141
move to territorial system, 103, 126–127
need for, 78
objectives, 139
opportunities for improving R&D credit rules, 61–62
proposed legislation, 91
prospects, 6, 145
R&D provisions, 48–49, 84, 96–97
response of trading partners, 91–94
royalties, 97
statutory corporate tax rate, 6
for technological future, 78
trade effects, 93–94, 140–141
Repatriation of earnings, 2, 11–12, 115
after TRA86, 122
cross-crediting practices, 122
forms of, 115
practice among U.S. multinationals, 35, 41
Residence-based taxation, 1
definition, 40
for optimal global production efficiency, 25–27
U.S. policy, 40
Residual tax rate, 67
Royalty income, 5–6, 35
as foreign income, 41, 42
foreign-source income of U.S. firms, 49
R&D expense allocations, 42, 45–46, 66
tax reform proposals, 97
U.S. tax rules, 95–96

**S**

Sales tax, 91
Saving-Exempt Income tax, 127

Section 1.861–8, 43–45, 72
Section 1.861–17, 72
Section 904(g), 72–75
Section 956A, 72
Sections 951–964, 78
Social rate of return, 53
Source-based taxation, 27, 111
State tax systems, 18
Subsidiaries, foreign, 2

**T**

Tariffs
free trade theory, 21–22
rationale, 22–23, 31–32
Tax havens, 19–20
global costs, 33
policy mechanisms, 32–33
rationale, 32
rationale for intervention, 33–34, 36
Tax policy
capital-export/-import neutrality, 113, 121
competitiveness goals, 88–89, 111–112
conceptual evolution, 134–137
conflicts among objectives of, 113
constancy and consistency, 6, 71, 83
depreciation of R&D expenditures vs. immediate deductibility, 59
economic efficiency goals, 88, 110–111, 121
effectiveness of R&D rules, 59–60, 62, 63
evaluation of free trade compatibility, 29–36
for global production efficiency, 25–27, 111
impact on foreign direct investment, 17–20
impact on R&D cost structure, 55–59
impact on R&D investment, 54
investment location decisions affected by, 67–68, 71
motivation for reform, 137–139
objectives, 39, 88, 110
opportunities for improving R&D rules, 61–62